YOU CAN TRUST HIM

ANCHORING YOUR HOPE IN GOD DURING DIFFICULT TIMES

JOAN E. MURRAY

Book cover designed by, Woodson Creative Studio.

Joan Murray Ministries & Seeds Of Hope Worldwide Missions

26340 FM 1736

Waller, TX 77848

281-398-2501

PRAISE FOR YOU CAN TRUST HIM

Joan walks the walk and talks the talk! I have witnessed this woman of God trust God over and over again for funds involving thousands of dollars to feed the poor in foreign countries. Even when the deadlines are often passed, she refuses to give up because God always comes through for her. Her faith and passion for God's work is a challenge to those of us in the ministry.

In her new book *"You Can TRUST Him,"* she shares a wealth of personal experiences and challenges; offers proffering solutions through the Word of God and His limitless grace to pull the Believer through. Oftentimes in our lives, we have a deep longing for total dependence on God, however, fast-growing societal inductions and the sense of responsibility make us refrain from the arms of the One we are meant to cast our cares on in utter self-abandonment.

Man was never made to be self-dependent, but God-dependent as evidenced in the Garden of Eden. God made everything ready in Eden before man was created. Our experiences, society, and civilization have bewitched mankind into thinking that self-sufficiency is a yardstick to measure human responsibility and freedom.

Joan has placed in our hands valid eternal keys to relinquish our cares and firmly trust in the God who now doubles as our loving Father. He never fails. This is a must-read for all Believers of our Lord Jesus Christ, regardless of level of spirituality; who are going through difficult times, anxiety, discouragement, and seeming failures in expectations. Meditate and apply these scriptural principles that will guarantee the evident manifestation of God's mercy and graciousness.

Reverend (Dr.) Isaac Egbewole
Lifetime Missions, President
Atlanta, Georgia

God gives us exactly what we need, right when we need it. We often forget His ways are not our ways. Whether He chooses to speak to us through His Word, circumstances or other people, one thing is for sure, YOU can trust Him.

Life can be hard, especially when facing a situation that seems impossible. For instance, while in the process of writing my own book, I was invited to read Joan Murray's book, *"You Can*

TRUST Him." It is a great honor and privilege to review a work of the heart before it hits the press. Therefore, in no way would I decline the offer. During the most difficult times of reliving and penning my own lifelong struggles and disappointments, God used Joan Murray and her wealth of biblical knowledge and wisdom to calm and reassure me through the darkest reflections of my life. Every chapter of this book delivered encouragement and insight of how God uses us for His Glory, not ours. Example after example, whether using biblical characters, other people or herself, Joan clearly demonstrates that each of us can trust God.

Kat Arnold
Kat Arnold Ministries,
(Bought, Caught & Released),
Author, Speaker
Shreveport, Louisiana

We were and are thrilled to be a part of the launch of this new book. As Pastor and wife, Joan has been a tremendous blessing to our ministry and proven to be a genuine friend. We are thankful for this wonderful book, *You Can TRUST Him*. It has truly been a blessing. I was in my waiting room season with God, when I received an email entitled, "You Can TRUST Him." The very first chapter spoke to my heart. It told me God sees me, and I am never invisible to Him. During my time of sickness and sorrow, God sees me. Reading this book renewed my strength to continue on this journey that He has me on. I will continue to pray with an unwavering faith knowing God sees me, and He is fighting for me because I am loved by Him each and every day.

This book is a testament to Joan's spiritual acumen as a teacher and student of the Word of God. Her insights and delivery speak both to the layperson and leaders, and offers encouragement to the like. Her writing style effectively communicates the message of Jesus, and her knowledge is evident of a life of devotion and faith. She doesn't just write it but she lives it. Your life will be blessed by this book as was ours.

Pastor Lucious & First Lady Mary Buggs
Fellowship MBC
Houston, Texas

I gained a deeper understanding of the Bible as I read, *You Can TRUST Him*. I found I wanted to keep reading because Joan was able to write with clarity that I had never understood before. I found myself feeling what Hagar, Sarah, Leah, and so many others were feeling as I read their stories. Joan explained in an interesting way why people behaved as they did and I felt like I was walking in their shoes. I also have a deeper understanding I can trust God, and I don't have to be perfect. God will love me anyway. I also came away with the hope God will answer my prayers, in His timing.

Thank you, Joan Murray, for writing this book. I believe after reading your book it will inspire others to want to read the Bible for themselves.

Kathy Coleman

Author, Illustrator, Speaker

Katy, Texas

As I read Joan's book, "You Can TRUST Him," I was reminded of the scripture in Romans 15:4, "Whatsoever things were written aforetime were written for our learning, that we through patience and comfort of the scriptures might have hope." Joan has done a great job of leading us through several of 'the things that were written' to bring light and understanding of the scripture and of our own selves as well. If any reader will rely on the Holy Spirit to guide, as you read this book, you will be much encouraged and find solid confidence that You Can TRUST Him.

Curtis A. Nestegard

Ambassador-at-large, India Gospel Outreach

Katy, Texas

ACKNOWLEDGMENTS

I thank the Lord Jesus Christ for His inspiration, leadership, and guidance in writing this book. I am always amazed by His inspiration as I write. The Holy Spirit always reminds me I am the note-taker, and He is the writer, so I can trust His directives.

I thank my Board of Directors, the Joan Murray Ministries, and Seeds of Hope Worldwide Missions Teams for their continued support, encouragement, and prayer each time I undertake another assignment to write the words the Lord gives me.

My sincere thanks to, Reverend Isaac Egbewole, Kat Arnold, Pastor Lucious & First Lady Mary Buggs, Kathy Coleman, and Curtis A. Nestegard for their time and commitment in reading and endorsing this book.

Thanks to Julia Rigos, and a few friends who helped to make this book better because of their edits. My thanks to David Meade and Rosalinda Garza for their wonderful contributions to this book.

To my family and friends, thanks for your support and encouragement in the writing of this book.

Thanks to the supporters of Joan Murray Ministries and

Seeds of Hope Worldwide Missions for your prayers and help as we take the gospel around the world.

CONTENTS

INTRODUCTION

I have entitled this book, *You Can TRUST Him* because some of us struggle with trusting God during difficult seasons. Many times, over the years I have struggled with trusting God, and have often failed to trust Him during some crucial moments.

Have you ever wondered why we struggle with trusting God when we so readily trust people? Negative experiences and disappointments in life can erode our trust in God. Some of us may secretly blame Him for allowing us to face difficulties; therefore, we lack trust in His ability to help us. Proverb 3:5-6 says, "Trust in the Lord with all your heart and lean not on your own understanding; in all your ways acknowledge him, and he will make your paths straight."

I had a conversation with a friend who shared that when she was younger, she trusted God for everything and with everything in her life, yet as she has gotten older, she realized she struggles to trust Him as she once did. When we struggle with trusting God it's often because people in our lives whom we trusted, failed us. We thought they had our backs and could be trusted but, they let us down. Unfortunately, some of us have projected or transferred these thoughts and feelings toward God. Some may reason since the people who should love and care for us have failed, God will do the same. He absolutely will not fail you. Numbers 23:19 says, *"God is not a man, that he should lie, nor a son of man, that he should change his mind. Does he speak and then not act? Does he promise and not fulfill?"* The answer is a resounding NO. God cannot lie even if He tried. His nature is absolute truth.

We fail to trust God at times because we are disappointed with Him. Why? Usually, it's because He did not answer our prayers exactly as we prayed or when we prayed. The loved one died; the healing has not yet come; the divorce happened; we lost our family; and after praying we still got laid off from the job. See, our expectation of what God should have done did not match the reality of what happened. When this happens, it causes doubt to filter into our hearts and erode our trust.

Question: What happens when our expectation of Jesus is not what He performs in our lives? Discouragement sets in and we may question the reality of who He is. Our expectation of what He should have done can cause us to have some setbacks when it does not manifest. However, even when He does not answer the way you expect Him to, you can still trust Him. God is faithful and trustworthy, and He is always working on your behalf. In your disappointment, you must make the appropriate adjustments to your emotions even though this can be difficult in moments of uncertainty. Jesus understands your struggles with doubt and unbelief. He welcomes your questions. He tells us in Isaiah 1:18, "*Come now, and let us reason together, says the* LORD: *though your sins be as scarlet, they shall be as white as snow; though they be red like crimson, they shall be as wool.*" He wants you to come and reason with Him. The King of the Universe desires to meet with you, to hear your heart on the matter. He invites you into a one-on-one intimate conversation with Him. As you grow in Him and come to know how faithful He is, Jesus will reveal to you He is Lord, even when you are facing tough times. You can trust Him.

Isaiah 40:28-31 says, "Do you not know? Have you not heard? The Lord is the everlasting God, the Creator of the ends of the earth. He will not grow tired or weary, and his understanding no one can fathom. He gives strength to the weary and increases the power of the weak. Even youths grow tired and weary, and young men stumble and fall; but those who hope in the Lord will renew their strength. They will soar on wings like eagles; they will run and not grow weary, they will walk and not faint."

This scripture reminds us of who God is and what He does in our lives. He never gets tired of hearing our concerns when we seek Him. He strengthens us when we feel like giving up because we cannot see a clear path to victory. He tells us as we anchor our hope in Him, He will not only renew our strength but, we will soar on wings like eagles. In ancient Hebrew culture, eagles were revered as mighty warriors who cared deeply for their young. Eagles are known for their strength and courage. They soar above dangerous storms to safety. In Exodus 19 when God delivered Israel from the Egyptians, He gave Moses a message for His people: *"You yourselves have seen what I did to Egypt, and how I carried you on eagles' wings and brought you to myself."* God will carry you through all the difficulties of life and bring you directly into His presence just as He did the Israelites. As you remain faithful to Him, He will cause you to mount up on wings like eagles, which is *'alah'* in Hebrew and means to go up, to ascend, or to go up over a boundary. God will give you strength and courage to rise above every stormy event in your life. He tells us in 1 Peter 2:6 that when we trust Him, we will never be put to shame.

The book you hold in your hands is filled with biblical examples and stories of modern-day men and women who, in the middle of devastating hardships, chose to trust God. As you study the lives of Hagar, Jeremiah, Caleb, John the Baptist, the woman with the issue of blood, Mary Magdalene, and Leah, just to name a few, you will find even when they struggled with trusting God, He showed up powerfully in their lives and gave them victorious outcomes. May their stories of anchoring their trust in Him during difficult times encourage you He CAN be trusted in your situation.

Don't give up. You can, indeed, trust Him to defend, rescue, and deliver YOU.

Joan E. Murray

OTHER BOOKS BY:

JOAN E. MURRAY

Boldness in Christ

Broken, Yet Unstoppable

Called and Chosen for Destiny

Discovering God Vol. 1

Discovering God Vol. 2

Faith That Conquers

Flow Through Me, Lord

Freedom In The Son

Hope In Difficult Seasons

I MUST PRAY

Lord, Make Me Whole

Overcoming Loneliness and Aloneness

Reconnect

Señor, Hazme Íntegro

Show Me How to Love

Time in Life's Waiting Room

Winning In The Battles of Life

Worship, Our Deepest Need

You Can TRUST Him

GOD SEES ME

It is inconceivable, but some of us have experienced times in our lives when we have felt as if we were invisible to others; times when we were overlooked because someone did not see our value.

We were invisible to these people because they may have had a greater status than us, or they simply felt they were better in some ways than we were. During these times we must remember who we are, and in whose image we are created. Your value is not in what you do, what you own, what you can contribute to others, or even in your vocation, it is in the fact that you are a child of the King of Heaven. God, through the death of His Son, Jesus, has adopted us into His family and given us the highest place of honor in Him. When you truly understand this, you will be able to shake yourself free from the shackles the enemy and other people may attempt to place on you.

> *Romans 8:16-17 says, "The Spirit Himself testifies with our spirit that we are God's children. Now if we are children, then we are heirs—heirs of God and co-heirs with Christ; if indeed we share in his sufferings in order that we may also share in his glory."*

Let's start by tackling what it means to be adopted and then we will talk about our inheritance as an heir of God. Biblical adoption is entirely different from our modern-day adoption. Adoption in ancient times was not for the benefit of the child but was to preserve the family name and legacy. It was to provide the family with a leader, someone who would become the head and lead them into the future. The adoptee received a new identity and became the same person as the adopter. During that century, a natural-born son could be disinherited, but a son by adoption could never be disinherited. Adoption means being accepted, embraced, welcomed, and to assume full responsibility for another.

In modern times, a person does not receive their inheritance until after the death of the parents, but not so in ancient times. The heirs, while their fathers lived, had joint control of their properties. Think about the prodigal son who asked for his inheritance and left home. He asked for and received it because it was already distributed to him and his elder brother while the father was still alive. In the Bible, an heir is someone who has been appointed to receive an inheritance. The above passage from Romans tells us we are heirs and joint heirs with Jesus. This means Jesus is the first-born Son, He holds the birthright and is the heir of all the Father has. Since God has given Jesus all of creation as a gift, which includes us, we have ownership with Him. Colossians 1:16 tells us all things were created for Him. As co-heirs with Jesus, we have the privilege of sharing in His inheritance. This means we have the same access to the Father and all His blessings, including salvation, and eternal life. We receive our inheritance through faith in Christ's sacrifice. Simply put, "We own all that Jesus owns." What good news for those who have been devalued by others.

When people treat us as if we are invisible, it can leave scars in our souls. I have experienced this yet, have also, unintentionally, overlooked others and been firmly corrected by the Holy Spirit. At the beginning of the ministry, when things were excessively slow, I went to an event and will never forget what happened, because it was painful. Although painful, it provided a lesson and a reminder for me concerning how to treat others. At this event, we were broken into subgroups. The leader of my group shared a prophetic word with me that went something like this, "God has a huge plan for your life and will open great doors for you. Even though things are not moving currently, there will come a day when you pick and choose what engagements to accept." This was such an encouraging word because the ministry journey had been such a struggle, with very few engagement opportunities. Later that day, I saw the group leader and approached her. I wanted to share with her how thankful I was for the word and present her with a copy of my first book. This is how she responded.

She was talking to one of her co-workers, so I stood a distance away in order not to overhear their conversation. The co-worker acknowledged me, but the group leader did not. She continued talking for an inordinate amount of time to her co-worker, who several times attempted to stop their conversation because I was waiting. The lady refused to stop talking or even acknowledge me, which made the person she was talking to visibly uncomfortable. I stood there, a while longer, then walked away in total disbelief that I had been treated so discourteously. Naturally, this hurt.

Even though I am a person who knows my value, and is secure in who I am, this left an indelible mark on my soul during the difficult ministry journey. It was painful to be over-looked and dismissed as if I had no value. This lady acted as if I was invisible and therefore treated me as though I was!

Later, the Holy Spirit reminded me of an instance a few years earlier when I worked for corporate America. I was an Event Planner and was working with a group of doctors in Cape Cod, Massachusetts. The staff and I were in the hotel head-quarters holding a meeting when a cleaning lady asked permission to clean the room. Since we were about to leave, we invited her in. One by one we began to leave the room, and I was the last one to leave.

As I prepared to close the door behind me, the Holy Spirit whispered these words to me, "Did you see the lady that came into the room?" I thought it was a curious question; of course, I saw the lady. He then asked, "Did you speak to her?" He knew I had not spoken to her, so I responded, "No Lord." I instantly got the message He was delivering to me and reopened the door. I went back into the room, greeted the lady, introduced myself, asked her name, and thanked her for her service. I had unintentionally overlooked her, and God wanted to make sure I corrected my behavior.

All of us in our busyness had overlooked this lady who was precious to God. I was gently reminded, by the Holy Spirit, how valuable each one of His creations is, and to make sure I attached the same value to them, no matter what their vocation or status in life. He told me a person's vocation did not define them; they were defined by who He created them to be. I was reminded we do not know what we will become; so to attach value to each person I meet. There was no malicious intention in us ignoring the lady, we were simply too caught up in ourselves and our duties to notice her. She was invisible to us. Even though we did not see her, God saw her and knew her.

God taught me this lesson early because He knew what my assignment was in His kingdom, a person He would use to take the gospel message around the world and to serve in some of the poorest countries and communities on earth. Imagine if I had not heard and responded to His prompting. I believe I could have unintentionally disqualified myself from some of the assignments He had for me. In every community we serve, we need to *see* each person; taking time with each one, reminding them God has not forgotten them, and they are deeply loved by Him. We are His hands and feet to the forgotten ones, and we bring His hope to the hopeless.

If today, you feel as if you are invisible to others, understand this, "God sees you!" His eyes are constantly on you. He knows where you have been. He is aware of every challenging life situation you have faced and are facing. He will never abandon you and will rescue you. Hold on a little longer, your King will rescue and help you even in the midst of being wounded by others.

God Is with You

Throughout the Bible you will find instances where people felt abandoned, and, in most cases, cried out to God for help. Remember in Mark 15:34 when Jesus was on the cross after taking our sins. At one point, He cried out, "My God, my God, why have you forsaken me?" Did God really forsake Jesus?

No. He did not, but during that painful time, Jesus felt God's absence so profoundly, that He cried out in agony. After crying out Jesus shows us He recognized God was still there. In Luke 23:46 He said, *"Father, into your hands I commit my spirit."* Not his body, His spirit. The part of Him that was eternal and everlasting. Jesus knew God saw Him and would resurrect Him. Not once during His suffering did God ever forsake His Son. He simply waited until the appropriate time, early Sunday morning, to raise Him from the dead. At times, we might feel as if God has abandoned us because we are not seeing answers to our prayers. As with Jesus, He has not abandoned you, even if it looks like He is not responding to you the moment you pray. Let's look at a story that demonstrates God's faithfulness even to those who are considered the least in our society.

There are times in our lives when things may appear extremely dim, and we cannot see our way clearly. In those moments we are challenged to remember God is a very present help in times of trouble (Psalm 46:1).

It often feels as if we are invisible not only to those around us but, also to God. While others may overlook us, God never overlooks us. He sees us. As I share the story of Hagar with you, I want you to focus not only on what God did for her but to see clearly that the same God who rescued her will come to your defense and aid.

We are introduced to Hagar while she is living as a slave in Abraham and Sarah's house. She was Sarah's maid and an Egyptian. Genesis tells us there was a famine in the land of Canaan and because of this famine Abraham and his wife, Sarah, went to live in Egypt. This famine was a test of Abraham's faith. Would he trust God to provide during this difficult season? Abraham failed to trust God, so they ended up in Egypt where they lied to the pharaoh saying Sarah was Abraham's sister. Sarah was very beautiful, and Abraham was afraid he would be killed because of her beauty. Prior to going to Egypt, it is evident he did not consult with God. As a result of their lie, the pharaoh had taken Sarah into his harem; therefore, God had to intervene and rescue her. Before the pharaoh could have intimate relations with her, God visited him in a dream and told him to return Abraham's wife to him or, suffer the consequences. He promptly returned her and asked Abraham to leave his country.

Even though Abraham lied, God did not allow him to leave Egypt empty-handed. He was recompensed generously by the pharaoh and was made wealthy because God was with him. Although Abraham had not made the best decisions, God blessed him anyway. Do you see it? Even when we do not consult God, and make wrong moves, God is still faithful to protect our lives from destruction because we are His. This does not mean we do not experience the consequences of our actions; it simply means God is there to see us through. His grace is sufficient for us.

Romans 8:28 tells us all things work together for good for those who love the Lord and are called according to His purposes. Abraham and Sarah saw the fulfillment of this scripture in their lives. As they left Egypt, however, Hagar went with them.

Hagar is now a servant in Abraham and Sarah's household. Her name means uncertain, and you will see this lived out in her life as we delve into her story. God had given Abraham a promise in Genesis 15 about a son who would become his heir.

After this, the word of the Lord came to Abram in a vision: "Do not be afraid, Abram, I am your shield," your very great reward. But Abram said, "O Sovereign Lord, what can you give me since I remain childless and the one who will inherit my estate is Eliezer of Damascus?" And Abram said, "You have given me no children, so a servant in my household will be my heir." Then the word of the Lord came to him: "This man will not be your heir, but a son coming from your own body will be your heir." He took him outside and said, "Look up at the heavens and count the stars—if indeed you can count them." Then he said to him, "So shall your offspring be." Abram believed the Lord, and he credited it to him as righteousness.

Genesis 15:1-6 (NIV)

Prior to the promise of an heir, Abraham decided to make Eliezer, his chief steward his heir, giving him his vast wealth, but God said no. God told Abraham He would give him a son and showed him the stars saying his children would be as numerous as the stars. This was a powerful promise from God, but it evidently was not enough to steady Abraham and Sarah while they waited for the manifestation. As they waited a long time without results, Sarah devised a plan to give her maid, Hagar, to Abraham so he could produce a son and heir through her. It is evident both Abraham and Sarah clearly heard God's promise of a son, but at this juncture, they had been waiting ten long years. As a result, her patience evaporated, she took matters into her own hands and caused a disaster in their lives. Listen, the seasons of waiting in our lives are used by God to prove what is in our hearts. What is also evident is Abraham's patience had also begun to wear thin because he did not stop Sarah and remind her of God's promise. He readily agreed with her and took Hagar as his wife. Hagar had no option but to obey her mistress and she conceived. This decision delayed the manifestation of God's promise in their lives for another thirteen years.

The decisions we make will have long-lasting effects on us and, also, on the generations to follow. I know, at times, we bemoan the excessively long wait for their promised son that Abraham and Sarah experienced but, let me propose something to you. Is it possible that because they decided to interfere with God's plan and produce their own promise, they lengthened their own waiting season? God gives the promise but there is always the journey and a process to get to the Promised Land.

As we wait on the manifestations of God's promises in our lives, we will be tested and tried. Our characters will be examined; our motives will be questioned and challenged. We will discover who we really are as we wait for God to move in our situations. Abraham and Sarah give us a perfect example of the cost of disobedience. There was great chaos and confusion in their home because, instead of trusting God, they took matters into their own hands.

After Hagar conceived, she became prideful. She began to despise Sarah and showed it. Sarah told Abraham about the situation and was given permission to discipline her. Some historians tell us Sarah's discipline was harsh. She made Hagar work extremely hard. Some say she even beat her. When we take matters into our own hands there are always consequences. Sarah hoped to gain a son by doing it her way instead of God's way. The consequences were extremely unpleasant. Hagar felt more powerful because God had blessed her instead of Sarah; she lost all humility and respect for Sarah. What Hagar forgot, though, was this—she was only the second wife to Abraham and Sarah always had first place. When Sarah's harsh treatment became unbearable, Hagar ran away from home and had a divine encounter with God. Let's examine her encounter.

The Angel of The Lord

The angel of the Lord found Hagar near a spring in the desert; it was the spring that is beside the road to Shur. And he said, "Hagar, servant of Sarai, where have you come from, and where are you going? I'm running away from my mistress Sarai," she answered. Then the angel of the Lord told her, "Go back to your mistress and submit to her." The angel added, "I will so increase your descendants that they will be too numerous to count." The angel of the Lord also said to her: "You are now with child and you will have a son. You shall name him Ishmael, for the Lord has heard of your misery. He will be a wild donkey of a man; his hand will be against everyone and everyone's hand against him, and he will live in hostility toward all his brothers." She gave this name to the Lord who spoke to her: "You are the God who sees me," for she said, "I have now seen the One who sees me."

Genesis 16:7-14 (NIV)

Hagar was one of only a few women who encountered an angel of God. She was one of approximately twelve people who met the angel of the Lord, the Lord Himself prior to His incarnation. Let's look at the other encounters with the angel of the Lord. In Genesis 13:14-15 after Abram and Lot separated, the Lord told Abram He would give him and his children all the land forever.

In Genesis 22:11-12 the angel of the Lord called Abraham out of heaven and told him not to slay his son. Again, in Genesis 31:11-13 we read the angel said to Jacob, *"I am the God of Bethel."* In Exodus 3:2-6 the angel told Moses in the flame of fire, *"I am the God of your Father..."* In Judges 6:11-12 the angel of the Lord appeared to Gideon and renamed him, calling him a mighty man of valor. In 2 Kings 19:35, the angel of the Lord killed 185,000 Assyrian soldiers and saved Jerusalem. He appeared to Abraham, Hagar, Moses, Joshua, and Balaam, to the Israelites, Gideon, Manoah, and Jacob.

The angel of the Lord was generally a messenger of good news but, at times, would also bring devastation. When He appeared, He accepted worship, as He did with Moses and Joshua. He told them to take off their shoes, for the place where they were standing was Holy Ground. Understand no regular angel will accept worship because they understand worship is reserved only for God and His Son. They alone are worthy to be worshiped by mankind. Therefore, this angel was the Lord Himself because He accepted the worship. In Malachi 3:1 God said about the first coming of the Messiah, *"Behold I am going to send my Messenger."* After Jesus became incarnate in the flesh, the angel of the Lord ceased appearing. Jesus, our Savior, is not an angel.

Hebrews 1:4 tells us He became as much superior to the angels as the name He has inherited is superior to theirs. John 1:1-14 tells us Jesus has existed from eternity. It is important you understand who Jesus is, our Savior, and not an angel.

When Hagar met the angel of the Lord she was a slave to Abraham and Sarah. I want you to absorb that statement. This clearly demonstrates the value God places on all people. He does not love us based on our stations in life but, based on who He created us to be. Hagar ran from Sarai straight into the presence of the God of the universe, while attempting to return to her homeland. The angel of the Lord found her by a spring and did something that reminds us of how God sees us. He addressed the slave girl by her name. He knew her. He asked where she came from and where she was going.

Unlike many others in the Bible who expressed great fear when they encountered angels, Hagar expressed no fear. The angel asked her these questions, although He already knew the answers. I believe in asking the questions, the angel was reminding Hagar who she was and her obligations to Abraham, Sarah, and her unborn child. The angel told her to return to Sarah and to submit to her. Pause and reflect on this: Knowing she faced great abuse and hardships, the angel told her to return and submit. She was to go back to Sarah and do what she was told. She was to surrender her own will and desires to Sarah. She was to obey the person who was making her life difficult. She was to clothe herself with humility, letting go of any prideful feelings, and submit to Sarah who did not see her value as a person, but only as a slave.

Submission is not a subservient position but, a position of great power and humility. The angel was not asking Hagar to do something impossible for her to do since it was already in her to submit. She had been submitting all along but, veered off course when she was promoted to the position of second wife and became pregnant.

Jesus submitted to all earthly authorities although He was

the Son of God. We are wired to submit as He did. Along with the direction to submit, Hagar was given an amazing promise. The angel told Hagar he would increase her descendants and they would be too numerous to count. Listen: God had spoken these same words to Abraham years earlier about the promised son, Isaac. He gave the same amazing promise to Hagar about her son even though he was not the promised heir, but because he was Abraham's seed. God had made a promise to bless Abraham and all his descendants, and Hagar's son was a descendant. God always keeps His promises no matter who we are, whether slave or free. God named her son, Ishmael, which means "God hears." He told her his nature would be a wild donkey of a man who would war against all his brothers. Armed with this promise Hagar returned home and submitted herself to Sarah.

God will always take care of those who are disadvantaged. God had seen Hagar's punishment, heard her cries for help, and He intervened. The slave girl had a face-to-face conversation with the Lord. She discovered, that even though she was not one of His chosen people, like Sarah, He was still aware of her and was moved with compassion because of her plight. Hagar encountered God in a way Sarah never did. Sarah never had a face-to-face meeting with the Lord. She did not hear God's promise for her son spoken directly to her from God's mouth; God had spoken it to Abraham, her husband. She overheard the conversation and laughed because she was too old. Hagar heard the voice of the Lord and had an intimate conversation with Him. I am painting a picture for you because God cares about everyone, no matter our stations in life. Out of a heart filled with gratitude and thankfulness, Hagar gave God a name, "You are the God who sees me." The Creator of the universe knew her name. He did not look down on her because she was a slave but showed her how valuable she was to Him.

God saw her not as a slave but, as one of His creations, as someone who was in trouble and needed Him to intervene. He was very aware of where she was in the trials of her life. HE SAW HER!

Take comfort today in knowing God sees you. Just as He saw Hagar and comforted her, He will comfort you. When you are in the difficult seasons of life and God does not answer you right away, it may appear He has left you, but He has not. In Hebrews 13:5, God says, *"I will never leave you nor forsake you."* This is an awesome promise for your life. Earlier I shared Mark 15:33-34 with you, and it bears repeating. As Jesus hung on the cross and darkness covered the earth signaling the absence of God's presence, the agonizing cry of Jesus was heard. He felt such a profound loss that for the first time, during all the horror He suffered, He cried out in agony, *"My God, my God, why have you forsaken me?"* God did not forsake Jesus but, it felt like that to Him. For the eons of time He had existed, Jesus had never been separated from God, so this moment of separation was agony for Him. Three days later God showed us He was always with Jesus when He sent the angel to roll away the stone and free His Son.

Throughout the Bible, you will see many who fulfilled great destinies went through a process of waiting and growing in God. God never left them. He was with them each step of the way, just as He is with you in your trials and your journey towards your destiny. Years after Ishmael was born, God fulfilled His promise and gave Abraham and Sarah their son and heir. Travel with me through the pages of this book and the Bible to discover how God works through those who surrender to His plans and trust His perfect timing for their lives.

The Eviction

Now the Lord was gracious to Sarah as he had said, and the Lord did for Sarah what he had promised. Sarah became pregnant and bore a son to Abraham in his old age, at the very time God had promised him. Abraham gave the name Isaac to the son Sarah bore him. When his son Isaac was eight days old, Abraham circumcised him, as God commanded. Abraham was a hundred years old when his son Isaac was born to him. Sarah said, "God has brought me laughter and everyone who hears about this will laugh with me." And she added, "Who would have said to Abraham that Sarah would nurse children? Yet I have borne him a son in his old age."

Genesis 21:1-7 (NIV)

Hagar had Ishmael, and after fourteen long years, Isaac was born. Ishmael had been the only child in the household for years but, at a celebration for Isaac, Sarah found Ishmael mocking Isaac and demanded Abraham put both Hagar and

Ishmael out. I do not find any place in the scriptures where Ishmael physically hurt Isaac, only this taunting of him. He mocked him, which means he teased him, poked fun, laughed at him, and ridiculed him. As the older brother, he should have known better. Sarah witnessed this and instantly told Abraham to get rid of that woman and her son. She did not even call them by their names. What happened to cause her to use such derogatory terms to describe Hagar and her son whose birth she had initiated? Do you remember the angel had instructed Hagar to return and submit to Sarah? I am sure Hagar did just as she was told and was obedient to Sarah all those years, but it is evident Sarah still resented Hagar for being the woman who gave Abraham his first son. The nature of this eviction was extremely harsh and seemed filled with unforgiveness towards Hagar and Ishmael. It appears Sarah was simply waiting for the moment after she received her blessing to get rid of Hagar and Ishmael. Yet even in this difficult situation, God was working on Hagar's and Ishmael's behalf.

Here is what I see in this passage. God, who knows all things, also knew what would happen the moment Isaac was born. Sarah would get rid of Hagar and her son, so God gave Ishmael fourteen years with his father, to be trained and groomed into manhood. By the time they were evicted, he was a young man who could handle adult responsibilities. During that century, men were adults at a much younger age than today. Ishmael was at an age where he could marry and have a family. As we look at this situation, we can see one clear reason why God often delays us even after we have prayed for a long period of time. He is always working on more than one thing in our lives and the lives of others. Often, our decisions not only affect us but others as well. Sarah's decision would affect Abraham, Hagar, Ishmael, Isaac, and even her.

Abraham struggled with the request to evict his son and second wife, but God reassured him and told him to do what Sarah asked. God told Abraham Ishmael would become a nation, and this promise was very similar to the promise given about Isaac. Remember fourteen years earlier God had given Hagar a promise of who and what her son would become. I don't think Hagar shared this promise with either Abraham or Sarah. I also think it is possible they did not even know she had run away and met the angel of the Lord.

God told Abraham what He had told Hagar about Ishmael's inheritance. This brought him the same comfort as it had Hagar years earlier. This promise assured Abraham his son would survive. Even though Ishmael was not the promise, he was still Abraham's seed and God had made a covenant to bless Abraham. Since God cannot lie, and His promises are true, these blessings were given to all of Abraham's seed. We are inheritors of these promises as well because we are also Abraham's seed.

Abraham sent Hagar and their son out into the harsh desert, after giving them water and some food. Consider how hard that must have been for Ishmael to lose his father, home, family, and friends all in one day. This must have been traumatic for him to experience this level of abandonment at such a young age. But even though Abraham had to abandon them, God never would! God became a father to the fatherless. Our choices can cause such pain and devastation in our lives. God in His infinite mercy always helps us.

As they began the journey home, to Egypt, Hagar's homeland, she got lost. It had been over twenty-five years since she had left home, so naturally, she could not remember the way. Abraham was very wealthy. He had servants, animals, and money, yet he sent them on their way with only food and water. He assigned no one to lead them home. Hagar could not find her way because she was overwhelmed and could not think clearly. After submitting to Sarah, who probably continued mistreating her, the reward for all her sacrifice was eviction. In addition to this, she lost her husband and her home in one day. She was now a single mother, which she never planned on being. She was heading home knowing she would have to explain to her family and friends what had taken place during all those years away.

The shame and embarrassment she faced were unbearable. Her life was spinning out of control. I invite you to walk in her shoes for a moment. How would you have handled this devastation? Would you have been emotionally strong during these difficulties? Would your mind have been clear enough for you to figure out how to get home? She was only human, and deeply wounded by this abandonment and rejection; therefore, could not see her way clearly. To top it all off, she had run out of water. God in His infinitive mercy came to her rescue a second time.

During this horror, she gave up, sat down, and turned away from her son so she would not see him die. Hagar, once again; had come to the end of herself. She was in a crisis and this time she had the additional responsibility of her son. Fourteen years earlier she was pregnant; this time her son was with her, and she did not know how to save him. She appears to have forgotten the promise God had given her fourteen years earlier that her son would be a great nation. The only way he could accomplish this was to stay alive. Hagar and Ishmael both began to cry. Amid hopelessness, most of us will cry out. The ability to cry helps to release pent-up emotions. Their cries were a recognition they were about to die and were helpless to do anything about it. The moment they began to cry, God responded.

Once again, the slave girl was introduced to the King of Heaven. Her second encounter with the Lord was different from the first. This time the Lord did not meet her face-to-face but spoke to her from heaven. She encountered God in a new way and had access to heaven. As with the first encounter, God asked her what was wrong. He comforted her because He knew she was fearful of her son dying.

God not only heard her cry but, the cry of her son as well. Since God had named him and given him a purpose, God would not allow him to perish in the desert. God not just responding to Hagar's cry but, also to the cry of this son of Abraham. By virtue of who his dad was, Ishmael was now an heir who received the blessings that were in Abraham's life.

God showed up in his life to address his needs. Do you see it? God loves all His creations. He does not want a single person He created to perish but for everyone to have eternal life (John 3:16).

Do you remember God named him Ishmael? Do you recall

the meaning of his name? I told you earlier in the chapter it meant, "God Hears." How significant, for the entire fourteen years of his life, each time someone spoke his name, they were speaking into his future—God would hear him. God's ways are far superior to ours (Isaiah 55:8-9).

The Lord told Hagar to take her son's hand and reminded her he would become a nation. He nailed down His promises to her once again. There was no doubting He would ever abandon them, and neglect to keep His promises. God had made Hagar these promises even though she had not yet claimed Him as her Lord. He loved her just as she was and gave her an opportunity to know Him as Lord. Amid their hopelessness, God was there. When all others failed them, He was a constant source of help. Those closest to them had cast them aside, yet God was there to lead them. He is always close to the broken-hearted and to those who are crushed in spirit (Psalm 34:18).

The scripture tells us God was with Ishmael as he grew. Think about that statement for a moment. God was a constant companion to the slave woman's son while they lived in a heathen country. He never left his side. He walked with him through the difficult days of manhood, through all his trials and temptations. God encouraged, supported, groomed him, and led Ishmael into the destiny he was created to fulfill. He became a father to the fatherless.

Psalm 27:7-10 says, "*Hear my voice when I call, O Lord; be merciful to me and answer me. My heart says of you, "Seek his face!" Your face Lord, I will seek. Do not hide your face from me, do not turn your servant away in anger; you have been my helper. Do not reject me or forsake me, O God my Savior. Though my father and mother forsake me, the Lord will receive me.*" He received Hagar and Ishmael and became a Father to them. The scripture tells us Ishmael married and became a great nation just as the Angel of the Lord had spoken.

Genesis 16:10, 12 tells us the angel of the Lord told Hagar He would increase her descendants so much they would be too numerous to count, and her son would be a wild donkey of a man; his hand would be against everyone and everyone's hand against him, and he would live in hostility toward his brothers. In Genesis 17:20, God told Abraham, concerning his son Ishmael, that He had heard his request to bless him, and He would surely bless him, make him fruitful, and greatly increase his numbers. God also said Ishmael would be the father of twelve rulers (tribes, princes).

Remember, through the lineage of Isaac, the son of promise, there are twelve tribes of Israel. Do you see how far God will go to keep His promise of covenant blessings in our lives even when we sin? Abraham had sinned and produced a child that was not in God's perfect plan for his life; yet, God still honored His Word exceedingly and abundantly above what Abraham could ever hope for concerning Ishmael. The prophecy for Ishmael was fulfilled. He married an Egyptian woman and bore twelve sons who became rulers over their respective tribes. Some historians believe many of the Middle Eastern people are descendants of Ishmael, Abraham's son. God kept His promise to Hagar and Abraham concerning their son and his future.

Some historians say Hagar never re-married, she remained faithful to her marriage to Abraham. Genesis 25:1 tells us

Abraham took another wife after Sarah died, whose name was Keturah.

Although Abraham had many more children after Ishmael and Isaac when he died, it was Ishmael and Isaac who buried him (Genesis 25:9). It is evident from this scripture there was contact between Abraham, Ishmael, and Isaac after Ishmael was evicted from their lives.

God takes care of His children. His eyes are always on us when we are broken and downtrodden in life. He is mindful of our struggles. When others overlook us; God sees us. We are not invisible to God. He does not look the other way when we cry out to Him but, watches over us and knows our struggles. There is never a moment in your life when you are invisible to God. He sees your value and has a plan to use your life for the greater good. If you allow yourself to believe people's lies about who you are, this can keep you from fulfilling your great potential in God. People do not define you, God does. Only God knows the seeds of greatness He has planted in your life. He is the only One who knows how to bring that greatness to the forefront. He knows the journey to your destiny and will be with you the whole time. I have discovered something—people often don't see your true value until they see God working in your life. Let me share a personal example with you.

When I was in my early twenties I had a lot of struggles, especially with unemployment. I was laid off from work at different times for several years. During the first two seasons of unemployment, I complained a lot. I did not know what God was doing. After interviewing for several jobs without success, I was stumped. During one of these difficult times, someone, whom I thought was a close friend, made the struggles even worse. She said, "I have known you for many years and it appears you are living for the Lord, but you keep having these struggles, so something must be wrong. Are there any secret sins in your life I don't know about that are keeping you in bondage?"

Imagine my dismay that someone whom I thought was in my corner, and understood my struggles, could believe I was without a job or finances to take care of my needs because I was sinning against God; therefore, He was punishing me. Before I could answer, she said, "I don't know how else to pray for you." I responded, "Don't pray, God has me covered." She did not understand, nor did I at the time, the difficult seasons were my proving ground. Let me explain. God was training me and pruning my life because He was preparing me for the future He had in store for me. These seasons of difficulties were a part of my journey to destiny. He was developing in me a deeper dependency and trust in Him. I would need it in the future to walk in the fullness of my assignments.

The friendship did not survive this pruning. Several years after starting the ministries and writing my first book, I saw her at an event. She said, "I have heard about your book and what you have been doing. I always knew God would use you." Talk about being amazed after hearing these words. She did not understand my struggles; therefore, she did not encourage me in them. God in His faithfulness showed her He was always with me. I was not, as she thought, suffering because I had done anything wrong, but because God had allowed the struggles to prove and test my heart and character. He was qualifying me for greater service in Him. Today, if people see your struggles and criticize you, remember they only see from a bird's eye view and not from an eagle's vantage point. Only God sees and knows all you will become. Forgive and release those who have abandoned you in the journey. Keep pressing into your future because it is filled with hope and blessings.

Before I close this chapter, here is a story that took place on a recent mission trip to Haiti and demonstrates God really does see us. While there, we visited and ministered to a group of beautiful disabled children at an orphanage. The first statement we heard from the Directors upon arrival was a bit appalling; they asked if we planned to stay and interact with the children. When I expressed surprise at the question, she told us many people simply drop off food and supplies but never take the time to meet and greet the kids. She stated people are often uncomfortable with the level of the children's disabilities, so they don't interact with them.

That was a very heartbreaking statement for the team and me to hear, and to process. The hours we spent with the children left a deep joy and fulfillment in our hearts greater than all the other places we had previously served. One of our team members, David Meade, had a profound encounter with a beautiful young girl who reminds me God sees us. Here is the story in his own words:

"I was able to go on a trip to Haiti with a local ministry the first week of November 2017 led by Joan Murray. On November 5th, 2017, our team of fourteen had an opportunity to visit an orphanage called Norte Maison. Norte Maison Orphanage takes care of mentally handicapped children either because they were born that way or because of severe malnutrition. Most of the 45 children who reside in Norte Maison have no records of their birth and have no ties to their families. It is where children go to be forgotten. Many of Norte Maison's children were found wandering the streets rummaging through trash cans for food.

As our team arrived, we were greeted by a friendly Haitian and American staff. They explained the story of how Norte Maison originated and gave general guidelines to our team as we entered the complex. The children were instantly happy we were there. Our team members played with the children, sang to them, and gave them cookies and candies, later we provided them with a warm lunch. The joy on their faces was worth the whole trip.

As I was walking through the compound taking pictures and grasping the reality of this place, I noticed a room tucked away in a corner. As I entered the darkened room, I saw about six baby cribs and one of the staff folding laundry. Out of the corner of my eye, in one of the cribs, I saw Sarah. This 7-year-old little girl was taken to the hospital a few years back due to severe seizures. The parents eventually left Sarah at the hospital and never came back. It was Haitian social services who had found Norte Maison and delivered her there.

Sarah's body was in a frozen state due to severe seizures. The volunteer staff picked her up out of the crib to show me, and her body stayed in complete form as if she was still lying in the crib—much like a corpse. My initial feeling was to leave the room because I was overwhelmed and uncomfortable being so close to human suffering, especially a child's suffering. As I left the room to go back to the group and the other kids, I felt convicted. I stopped in my tracks and wrestled with God, knowing what he was asking of me. In a complete inner tantrum, I turned around in my discomfort and asked the staff if they could place Sarah in her run-down, rusty, flat-tire, fly-infested wheelchair.

I pushed Sarah out to the courtyard where the team and the other kids from the orphanage were playing. Sarah was the only child there not in the group. I saw a shady spot in the courtyard where I could drop Sarah off, and continue taking the photos of the team and the other kids. I was looking for a way out and just wanted to hide behind the camera. In my mind, bringing Sarah out to the courtyard was good enough, but it wasn't good enough for God.

As I was fleeing externally and internally, God again was convicting me. Again, I was reluctant. However, God's resiliency was outmatching my reluctance, and with great discomfort I found myself sitting and holding Sarah, along with all the flies that swarmed around her mouth and eyelids. I held her as if I was holding a baby. Gently patting her and singing softly to her, I was reminded that my boys, Bernardo and Aston, were the same age as Sarah. How fortunate we truly are! I then became connected to what was really happening. God, at this moment, just wanted Sarah to feel loved as I loved my own boys.

As I was holding and singing to her, I felt the tense muscles that caused Sarah to be frozen like a corpse at ease, and her body relaxed. We sat there, in a moment that contained all moments, and enjoyed the cool breeze. God was with Sarah that evening. As I was holding her, her muscles were so relaxed they fell back to an almost normal composure. I saw her hands and noticed she was missing a finger, and half of another. The staff later explained that not too long ago, in one of her seizures, she had completely bitten off her fingers. In our time together, while Sarah was getting a needed break from tension, the staff observed in wonder her composure and how relaxed she had become.

It was time to leave the orphanage, and I was an emotional mess. In all of my travels, and all of my ministry, I was reminded that following Jesus always results in making the comfortable, uncomfortable, and the uncomfortable, comfortable."

God sees all His people. He sees us when we are strong and when we are weak.

He sees us when we are wronged and hurt by others, and He comes to our rescue. He sees the broken condition of mankind and is moved with compassion to help us. If you have not yet discovered that God is for those we call underdogs, I invite you to search the scriptures to see how He feels about the oppression of any people. He created them, so He sees them all.

Remember to take heart, my friend, God sees you!

Just like Hagar, you can TRUST Him!

BEFORE I FORMED YOU

Have you ever been in a tough season in your life where you had to endure some hard, difficult things? If you have, you may have discovered the key that enabled you to be victorious – perseverance.

Perseverance has been the cornerstone for many who have chosen a life of faith. It is necessary to have grit to get through tough times and perseverance is that grit. Without perseverance, many of us would give up when our way is paved with difficulties. If we give up, we will miss some of the greatest opportunities to know God and His Son in a rich and powerful way.

Perseverance means to abide, to endure, to persist, to remain steady in trials, and not to give up. Pause for a moment and review these definitions. Do you see your reflection in any of these words? Have you endured your hard seasons and trying times with patience? Have you remained steady and focused when you were overcome with trials and tribulations? Have you persisted while not being sure if you had the strength to continue? Let me share a secret with you. God knew all along you had all that was necessary to be victorious over these hardships. The enemy cannot send anything into your life that God is not fully aware of, and since He knows all things, He knows what you can handle. He also knows what difficulties will develop His character in you and showcase His power through you.

1 Corinthians 15:58 is one of my favorite scriptures. It says, *to be steadfast, immovable, always abounding in the work of the Lord for you know your labor is not in vain in Him. The scripture tells you to be steady; to let nothing move you; to stay the course because you are not laboring in vain.*

In everything you face, God is with you and will give you a victorious end. Perseverance is not a one-time event; it must become a lifestyle. It is something you will need to do continually if you are determined to succeed. Those who persevere will succeed because they refuse to give up. Our Christian life is a race to the finish line; we are not aimlessly running around as if we have no destination in mind. In any race, the one who persists, who never gives up in the face of difficulties, will always triumph. Here is a perfect example.

A few years ago, we went to Zimbabwe to minister and to do missions. As is our usual practice, we visited a children's hospital to pray for the kids and to bless them with gifts. While we were going through the wards, I came across this little girl who was about eight years old. She went from one person to another saying hello and smiling and constantly singing. She seemed healthy and so very joyful. When I asked her if she knew Jesus, her answer was an instantaneous and firm, yes. I then asked her to sing a song for me and she broke out into a song that brought a smile to all of our faces. Her parents watched her with smiles but there was also sadness in their eyes. I commented that she seemed healthy and asked why she was in the hospital. She was there because one of her legs had been amputated and it had developed an infection.

Throughout all her health challenges and the amputation, we were told she never lost her joy or her smile. Her spirit was infectious and contagious. Although there were many sick children in the ward, the joy of this one small child lit up the entire place. I pondered to myself then, and even now, how often I lack joy when facing difficult seasons. It is hard at times to find a smile, much less to encourage others.

This young girl was facing a lifetime of challenges in a country where so many healthy people struggle to survive, yet she embraced her difficulties by holding onto her joy. It is my hope and prayer she will always find her strength in the joy she exhibited. Nehemiah 8:10 tells us the joy of the Lord is our strength. I encourage you to find your joy in the hope that Jesus can cause you to triumph over all your troubles.

~

Glory in the Struggles

It is inexplicable, but there is glory in every struggle we endure and overcome. Let me explain. The word glory speaks of wonder, grandeur, fame, praise, success, triumph, and admiration. Even if no one knows the internal struggles you are facing, God knows. He sees you and will reward you for attaining the victory. Every struggle will birth something magnificent in you. Christ Jesus is being formed in you during the struggles (Galatians 4:19). Have you discovered yet that it is almost impossible to avoid difficult life situations? You cannot go around them; you cannot go over them; and you cannot go under them. You must go through them. Why is that? Life is filled with difficulties and hardships, and no one is exempt from them. They affect all races, and socioeconomic status. From the moment Adam and Eve sinned to this day, we have and will continue to face difficulties. It is a part of the fallen nature of man. Often, it is not the devil that creates problems in our lives; it is the decisions we make that can have the gravest impact.

Perseverance, however, is an essential part of the Christian's life. Jesus told us in John 16:33, that in the world we will have tribulations. 2 Timothy 3:12 says *"All who desire to live a godly life in Christ will be persecuted."* We will go through difficulties. Focus on these words—go through. Trouble and trials will not remain permanently in our lives. They will come but they will eventually pass away. In Hebrews 11, we find the stories of many heroes of the faith who overcame through perseverance.

Their examples testify to us that victory is attainable. Hebrews 11:13 tells us Abel, Enoch, Noah, Abraham, and Sarah, all died in faith without receiving all the promises. They saw the manifestations of their promises from a distance. Many of these heroes' lives were filled with great highs and deep lows. They endured some of what we are enduring today and were successful. Even though God did not deliver them immediately, they did not stop believing and persevering. They fought the good fight of faith and finished their races.

Romans 8:18-19 says, "*For I consider that the sufferings of this present time are not worthy to be compared with the glory which shall be revealed in us. For the earnest expectation of the creation eagerly waits for the revealing of the sons of God.*" 2 Corinthians 4:16-18 says, "*Therefore we do not lose heart. Even though our outward man is perishing, yet the inward man is being renewed day by day. For our light affliction, which is but for a moment, is working for us a far more exceeding and eternal weight of glory, while we do not look at the things which are seen, but at the things which are not seen. For the things which are seen are temporary, but the things which are not seen are eternal.*" Let's unpack these scriptures.

What is glory? The scriptures tell us glory is revealed in the struggles and in the waiting. The things we are suffering are preparing us for an eternal weight of glory. We experience the glory of God as a kind of weight. The original meaning of glory is to be heavy or to weigh upon. When we are in the presence of God's glory, we become conscious of something greater than ourselves. His presence is pressing upon us. It's crowding us and weighing on us like a heavy spiritual presence. That is why some people will fall down while being ministered to, because this weight is pressing down on them and they cannot stand up in His presence.

Let me share a personal example. A few years ago, I was in Honduras ministering at a Sunday night event. The people had been in church the entire day and the atmosphere was saturated in praise, worship, prayer, and thanksgiving. Unbeknownst to me, I had walked into an atmosphere that was charged with the power of God. After ministering, I invited people with needs to the altar. As the team and I ministered to them, God began to move. In one instance, as I got ready to pray for a young boy who was sick, I began to topple over. One of my team members, who was working with me, quickly realized I was about to fall over and grabbed my jacket to keep me upright. I continued ministering in that condition because I could not seem to get my legs to function. After the ministry time, I needed help to get to my seat. When it was time to get on the bus and head back to the hotel, I still needed help. The weightiness of God's glory was so powerful in the service I was overcome with it. It took a while to recover. Although I have felt this at other times since then, it has never been to that degree. The only way to explain it is that the weight of His glory sat on me. Many people were healed because He was present during the service. When we are in the presence of God's glory, we become conscious of something far greater than ourselves.

Romans 8 and 2 Corinthians 4 tell us something else about glory. They tell us afflictions do not merely precede the glory; they help to produce the glory in our suffering. Think about it.

How was Jesus glorified? It was as a result of His suffering. Jesus was given the highest place of honor because of what He suffered. His difficulties helped to produce a greater degree of glory in His life. Through His suffering, He glorified God, His Father. God would not have received the glory had Jesus not said yes to the anguish and suffering He endured before and on the cross. His suffering cannot compare to the glory He now enjoys. This also holds true for us.

Our suffering is minor compared to what God wants to produce in us. Even though some of you may be experiencing what the scripture calls a wasting away, our inner self is being renewed daily in the Lord. The Bible tells us what we are suffering is a light momentary affliction and it is being used to prepare us for an eternal weight of glory that is without comparison. I know your struggles do not feel light to you. They are painful and hard. Yes, but when compared to what Jesus suffered, they are indeed light.

In your struggles, allow the power and presence of Jesus to become formed in you. The heroes of the faith refused to give up even though they were beaten, ridiculed, thrown in dungeons, faced lions, and thrown into fiery furnaces. They stood in the face of great obstacles, facing each trial or difficulty in God's strength. They considered their suffering to be worth it since they were winning souls for the Savior. We can imitate them by walking in their footsteps. I encourage you to keep the vision of the glory God is receiving out of your struggles, squarely in front of you, so you are motivated to keep pressing forward and to not give up.

Proverbs 24:16 says, "Though a righteous man falls seven

times, he will get up, but the wicked will stumble into ruin." You can get up again. I know it does not feel as if you can, but you have what is needed deep in your soul to rise above every difficult circumstance.

∼

How Do I Persevere?

It sounds easy for me to tell you to persevere, but how do you do it? You do it by refusing to quit, refusing to give up, by setting a goal before you and making it your focus. You must have a reason for the hope you have. That reason is how you will overcome and be victorious. The reason why you are persevering will be what drives you and keeps you from quitting. Along the journey, you will be challenged, questioned, and at times harassed by the enemy, but remember your goal. That goal will keep you moving forward. As you are persevering, some people will question your motives and why you keep trying in the face of impossibility. They will not understand your determination and it is okay because they don't know your vision. Each of us has a journey we must take to get to our destiny. Often the journey can be painful and heartbreaking to those who are watching our difficulties. They simply do not understand our struggles and why we must keep going.

As you study the Bible, you will find many people, including Jesus, who had difficult journeys in reaching their destinies. Jesus' journey to His destiny was the cross. Joseph's journey was a prison. David was on the run for his life for approximately thirteen to fifteen years before ascending to the throne. Moses was in hiding for forty years before being used by God. You get the picture, right? We are being formed into the image of Jesus Christ in the journeys of our lives. These seasons are designed to test our characters, our integrity, and our morals. They help to qualify us for greater purposes in the kingdom. The prophet Jeremiah had a difficult journey, but he fulfilled an amazing destiny. He was God's mouthpiece! What an honor to be used in such a powerful way.

Joy is coming!

Psalm 30:5 tells us "Weeping may endure for a night, but joy comes in the morning." How many of you have wept over difficult life's struggles? You have had some painful seasons and at times may have wondered if you would recover. I think of many people who have faced sicknesses, the deaths of loved ones, financial struggles, and relationship struggles—hard difficult things; yet, they are still standing. At times, as you were going through, you may have wondered if you would make it. God has put in you the amazing power and strength of the Holy Spirit to stabilize you during these times. He is your rock and your place of refuge in the raging storms. That is why we must cultivate an intimate relationship with Him; so we know where to go for help when life is at its most painful. You can be assured of this—God will see you through. Many of us have wept over disappointments in our lives and wondered if we would ever experience joy again; eventually, however, the joy did return. As you face one storm after another, you may wonder if the sun will ever shine again for you.

The answer is a resounding YES! Not only will the sunshine again, but the SON, through His sacrifice on Calvary has guaranteed joy will come in the morning (Psalm 30:5).

If there is anyone in the Bible who persevered through great hardships, it was Jeremiah. In Hebrew, his name means, 'May Jehovah exalt, or exalted by the Lord.' Looking at his painful journey one may conclude he was not exalted, but I beg to differ. Because of his steadfastness in the journey, and his victories over struggles, we are still hearing about him centuries later just because He endured. He stayed the course, doing the hard work because it was ordained for him by God. His goal was obedience to the One who called him.

Jeremiah's father was a Levitical Priest, and it was because of this childhood training for holy service, that God began grooming Jeremiah for his calling. According to Jeremiah 1:5, God had set Jeremiah apart before he was formed in his mother's womb. This means God knew him before he was born. It is evident Jeremiah and each of us existed with God before He gave us our earthly assignments. God called him while he was young, but Jeremiah told God he was too young and could not speak. In essence, he was telling God his assignment was too hard for him. An Israeli youth during that century would be between the ages of thirteen and eighteen.

His assignment, "Behold, I have put my words in your mouth, see I have this day set you over nations and over kingdoms, to root out and to pull down to destroy and to throw down, to build up and to plant." (Jeremiah 1:9-10). This was a high calling for such a young person, but God knew what was in him; even if he was unaware of it. The charge he was given was to proclaim the destruction and the rebuilding of nations that would eventually point people to the Kingdom of God. This assignment terrified Jeremiah, so he told God he was but a child. He was trying to find a way out; God had hemmed him in. God told him not to say he was a child but to go and speak what He commanded. He was not to be afraid because God was with him to rescue him. The mere fact the word 'rescue' is in the sentence tells us something.

Jeremiah would face hardships and would not be well received. God would come to his aid when He needed help. Did you notice God told him not to be terrified of the people? He could not fear the people he was serving and leading. This is a word for you today—don't be intimidated by what people will think or say about you, just be God's mouthpiece and He will handle the rest.

When God gives you an assignment, He equips you for the work. God began by asking Jeremiah some questions and was patient with his struggles. What do you see Jeremiah? God was not just asking about his natural sight but his spiritual insight. Sometimes we don't see all God is doing or can do because we are looking through natural lenses. Remember, God is Spirit, so we must get His spiritual perspective in every situation. Jeremiah saw a branch of an almond tree. God said, "Yes I am watching to see that my word is fulfilled." The Hebrew word for almond is shaked, and it means "to watch."

The significance of the almond tree is they are the first to wake up after winter and are known as "watching" trees—trees that watch for the approach of spring. It is amazing to see beautiful almond trees blossoming all over Israel every winter. They are the first trees to bloom and yet the last to bear fruit and to lose their leaves. By seeing the almond branch, God assured Jeremiah He was watching over His Word to bring it to pass, no matter how long it took. God used a natural example of the almond tree to confirm what He would do in Jeremiah's life—He would keep His Word. The lesson of the almond tree is God in heaven watched a sinful nation turn from Him and declared it would have consequences. The almond tree represents the speedy approach of God's judgment.

God asked again—what do you see Jeremiah? He saw a boiling pot tilting away from the north and God spoke a word to him. He said from the north disaster would be poured out on all who lived in the land. The steam of this boiling pot represented God's judgments, which are often compared to fire. The boiling pot signified the nation would be in great commotion and turmoil. Jeremiah's assignment was to report a great national calamity would break forth from the north, and this disaster would be poured out on all who lived in the land. Jeremiah was young, and the first assignment he was given by God spelled disaster for his people. No wonder he was terrified.

It is evident God was angry with His people and was about to destroy them. Why was He so angry with them? There was widespread idolatry by King Josiah's father, Amon, and his grandfather, Manasseh (2 Kings 21:10-20). In Jeremiah 44:19, we see the people promoted the vile practice of child sacrifices and the worship of some queen in heaven; therefore, God was angry with their grievous sins. 2 Kings 21:9-10, 20 says they committed more sins than all the nations God had destroyed before them

He used Jeremiah to reveal their sins to them along with the grave consequences they would suffer. In addition to all of this, the people were prideful, lacked gratitude toward God, committed idolatry, were adulterous, lied, slandered others, and broke the Sabbath, oppressed foreigners, orphans, and widows. Compare it to our society today; do you see these same sins being committed? YES! There is coming a day when our longsuffering God will have had enough of this sinful generation as well.

God is a just and righteous God. As much as He loves mankind/His creation, He must deal with the sins of the world. What you and I can be assured of, however, is He gives many opportunities for repentance before sending disaster. I am reminded of the story of Noah. Before sending the flood, the people had one hundred and twenty years to repent and turn to God but they did not. With all the evidence around them—the building of the ark; the animals being gathered into the ark; and Noah's testimony, no one said yes during all those years; so, they lost their lives.

There is a warning to our generation if we turn from wickedness, God will forgive us, but if we do not, then we must be ready to face His judgment. Do you know God would rather bless us than judge us? We only experience His judgment because we neglect to obey Him. As with the children of Israel, God allowed them to be under Babylonian captivity for seventy years because, they refused His instructions for living righteously, and consistently consorted with the enemies of God. They worshiped other gods and neglected the one true God who loved them. They suffered the consequences because of their consistent disobedience.

~

The Hardships of Ministry

Jeremiah experienced some severe hardships as he served God. He warned the people of the disasters that were to come, and his news was not well received. In Jeremiah 16, God forbids him to marry and have children. Why? God was protecting him, even though it did not appear as such. As God looked at the waywardness of Jerusalem and Judah, He told Jeremiah the parents of his generation would lose their children to deadly diseases. Listen to what else God told him *"These children would not be mourned, nor would they be buried by their parents," (Jeremiah 16:1-6).*

This is hard to believe unless something severe had transpired in their hearts. In addition, He said these kids would be like refuse (rubbish, garbage, junk) lying on the ground. He elaborated further saying these children would either die by the sword or by famine, and their bodies would be food for the birds. God did not want Jeremiah to have children and then suffer the same fate as the others. God was protecting him from heartbreak.

Other hard instructions for Jeremiah were he could not mourn, show sympathy, or even fellowship with these people;

he could only warn them of impending disasters. It is hard for most of us to comprehend why God allows such suffering and devastation. We wonder how any good can come out of it, but He always brings good out of disaster if we have eyes to see and ears to hear what He is doing.

When King Josiah died, Jeremiah's prophetic job became extremely hard. His messages caused great hostility from the people. He was beaten and locked up and had death threats because of what he said. Even his family conspired against and betrayed him. Jeremiah 12:6-8 says, "For even your brothers, the house of your father, even they have dealt treacherously with you; yes, they have called a multitude after you. I have forsaken my house; I have left my heritage; I have given the dearly beloved of my soul into the hands of her enemies. My heritage is to me like a lion in the forest; it cries out against me; therefore, I have hated it."

Jeremiah was not to believe a single word they spoke to him. Their words were smooth and did not hold one shred of truth. Jeremiah was mocked, ridiculed, and became the laughingstock of the nation. But he persevered. Now you may understand why he was known as the weeping prophet. His journey and assignments were hard. He saw disaster after disaster because the people would not repent and return to God. He watched the people's starvation and death due to the famine. He watched as invaders came in and destroyed them but was helpless to do anything because it was God's judgment against a wayward people. Only God could determine when enough was enough.

So, Jeremiah continued to follow God and to warn the people but, they turned a deaf ear to both him and God. Jeremiah 20:9 speaks of Jeremiah's devotion and steadfastness in his difficult assignments. The scripture says, "But if I say, I will not mention his word or speak any more in his name, his word is in my heart like a fire, a fire shut up in my bones. I am weary of holding it in; indeed, I cannot." Jeremiah had no option but to speak God's truth. With all his hardships, Jeremiah still could not stop prophesying, declaring God's name, and could not stop speaking God's words.

Pause for a moment and do some reflections on your hardships. Can you confidently declare what Jeremiah said, or, do you pull away from God when He allows trouble to come into your life? Do you blame Him for the troubles or, do you recognize the devil is the one who brings the trouble? When we pull away from our fellowship with God in times of difficulty, it is because often we blame Him. We reason since He is God and is all-powerful, He should have kept us from trouble. Some people are angry with God and others are disappointed with Him. Yet, instead of sharing their hurts with Him so He can remedy the situations; they turn away from Him while holding on to their offenses.

Unfortunately, these folks are simply going through the motions of Christianity; their relationships with God are not as solid as they once were. Jeremiah stayed close to God even though it hurt. He followed hard after God. He had moments of meltdowns and times he wished he was not born, yet he stayed connected to God and obeyed His directives. He kept prophesying; kept trusting; and kept persevering. He recognized even though God did not mitigate the disasters, He was still in control and would bring about the best outcome in the end.

During all the horror he faced, here is one of the greatest scriptures in the book of Jeremiah. Jeremiah 20:11 says, "But the Lord is with me like a mighty warrior; so, my persecutors will stumble and not prevail. They will fail and be thoroughly disgraced; their dishonor will never be forgotten." He had confidence God would bring him through. In the end, and much to their dismay, all his prophecies manifested in the lives of those in Jerusalem and Judah. God, however, gave Jeremiah a word that sustained him; it was the promise of restoration for the Jews. This promise brought him hope amid all his struggles.

God has a word for you, too. It is a promise of the great things He will do for you on the other side of your struggles. Like Jeremiah, you must hold on tightly when waves of difficulties are tossing you around. Know that in all the difficulties you face, God is your anchor in the storms. He does not bring the storms to your life, but He does use them for your growth, His glory, and to make a difference in the lives of others.

When hardships come, remember God is with you like a mighty warrior. Before God formed Jeremiah, He knew what he would become. Jeremiah simply had to say yes to God to attain victory, and he did. You, too, must say yes to Jesus even if the assignments appear to be difficult. God has deposited some significant seeds of greatness into your life that you may not yet have tapped into. He wants you to own them and give Him clearance to use you. God has already equipped you for everything He requires of you, and He knows what He is doing. He did not make a mistake when He chose you. His deposit of greatness into you is there so He can showcase you to the world and receive glory from your life.

What struggles do you face from day to day? As you devote yourself to service to God, how do you navigate the stormy trials? Have you discovered your greatest safety net is in God's presence? Have praise, worship, prayer, and the Word become your anchor during the raging storms? The only way to ultimate victory is to anchor your hope and trust in God. The quickest way to freedom and safety is to praise and worship Him while using the power tools of prayer and the Word to garner greater results in your life. Victory will come to you when you persevere and refuse to give up. You will prevail; you will triumph; you will see the goodness of the Lord in the land of the living. Keep this in mind—before He formed you in your mother's womb, He had already planted seeds of greatness in you, including the tenacity needed to fulfill all your assignments.

Remember, He is with you like a mighty warrior. He will see you through every struggle.

Just like Jeremiah, you can TRUST Him!

GIVE ME JUSTICE

How many of you can say there have been times in your lives when you needed God to give you justice? When no one else came to your rescue, God was with you, and He fought for you. There are seasons when we will come under attack because of our righteous stance. In those seasons, we must remember God can and will do battle on our behalf. Before you allow these challenging situations to overtake your emotions and lives, find your way into the presence of Jesus. Ask Him to intervene on your behalf because you cannot win without Him. True justice comes from God alone; for He is our Judge, and He is faithful.

Genesis 18:25 says, *"Will not the Judge of all the earth do right?"*

Throughout the Bible, we find God executed judgment over wrongs that were committed against Him and His people. He judges sin! Let's look at several examples of His judgments as recorded in the Old Testament: He judged Adam and Eve, then evicted them from paradise when they disobeyed Him (Genesis 3). During Noah's time, He destroyed the world with a flood because of the peoples' wickedness (Genesis 6-8). In Genesis 18-19, He destroyed Sodom and Gomorrah because of their abominations. He overthrew the Egyptians and drowned their army as they attempted to harm His people, the Israelites (Genesis 15:14, Exodus 14:26-31). In the short period of time Moses was receiving instructions from God about how to care for the people, they built and began to worship an idol; after all God had done to free them from bondage and provide for them. He destroyed those who worshipped the golden calf after He had delivered them from Egyptian bondage (Exodus 32:26-35).

In Joshua 7, when Achan sinned and stole items during a war, God destroyed him, his family, and all they owned because he had brought sin into the camp of the Israelites. One man's sin caused problems for every Israeli in the camp. God destroyed him because if He had not, others would have followed his example and many would have missed entering into their Promised Land. God judged and humbled Nebuchadnezzar because he was prideful and pompous.

God also dealt with injustice and unrighteousness in the New Testament. In Matthew 21:42-44, He dealt with the Jews because they rejected Jesus Christ, His Son.

Jesus said to them, *"Have you never read in the Scriptures: 'The stone the builders rejected has become the cornerstone; the Lord has done this, and it is marvelous in our eyes? ' Therefore, I tell you that the kingdom of God will be taken away from you and given to a people who will produce its fruit. Anyone who falls on this stone will be broken to pieces; anyone on whom it falls will be crushed."*

Matthew 21:42-44 (NIV)

In Acts 5:1-11, God killed Ananias and Sapphira when they lied to the Holy Ghost about the value of a piece of land they had sold. They plotted to misrepresent the exact amount of the sale to the Apostle Peter when they brought their gift. Their lies resulted in them dying instantly because they lied to the Holy Ghost, who knows everything, and were not lying to man. In Acts 12:21-23, King Herod sat on his throne wearing his kingly robes and the people began shouting, "The voice of a god and not of a man!" Immediately, upon hearing these words, an angel of the Lord struck him down; because he did not give glory to God. He was eaten by worms and later died. Herod was not a god, and so he experienced God's judgment for receiving the glory that only belonged to God.

In 1 Corinthians 11:29-32, we are told when we eat the bread and drink the cup of the Lord in an unworthy manner, we are bringing judgment onto ourselves. As a result of this many people are weak and sick among us and many sleep (die). The scriptures tell us if we judge ourselves we will not be judged.

Although God will ultimately judge us, He still gives us

opportunities to judge ourselves and to correct any wrong behaviors when we are overtaken by sin. We have all sinned and missed God's standards but He is still available to bring about our deliverance. Deuteronomy 27:19 says, *"Cursed be anyone who perverts the justice due to the sojourner; the fatherless, and the widow." And all the people shall say, "Amen."* The word amen means 'so be it', which means it is done. God has declared a curse on anyone who does not welcome the stranger, or take care of the orphans and widows. A curse is the opposite of a blessing and means destruction. It is a pronouncement of ill will or misfortune because a person opposes God and His plans. You can be assured of this: God will fight against anyone who oppresses those whom He cares about—poor, widows, orphans, and the aliens/strangers (Exodus 22:22-24).

In Luke 18, He did battle against an unjust judge, for a widow to whom the judge refused to give justice. Your God will fight for you and overthrow anyone who is attempting to hinder you. Let's look at the story of this widow and find truths about how God will battle on your behalf when people treat you unjustly. This widow was persistent because she knew God was on her side, and He would give her victory. This holds true for you as well, so keep fighting for what you deserve.

~

Stand Your Ground

If there is a time in your life to stand your ground, it is when people are treating you unjustly. As I just stated earlier in the chapter, God wants you to have justice when situations are unfair or unreasonable in your life. He does not want you to sit back and allow the devil and those serving him to trample over you and your values. He was not silent as he vigorously defended the widow. God will not be silent about you. Jesus wants you to keep praying and to refuse to give up when your pathway is paved with difficulties. He has your solution. He will make the devil pay for all the hardships he brings into your life.

Then Jesus told his disciples a parable to show them that they should always pray and not give up. He said: 'In a certain town there was a judge who neither feared God nor cared about men. And there was a widow in that town who kept coming to him with the plea, "Grant me justice against my adversary." For some time he refused. But finally he said to himself, "Even though I don't fear God or care about men, yet because this widow keeps bothering me, I will see that she gets justice, so that she won't eventually wear me out with her coming!" ' And the Lord said, "Listen to what the unjust judge says. And will not God bring about justice for his chosen ones, who cry out to him day and night? Will he keep putting them off? I tell you, he will see that they get justice, and quickly. However, when the Son of Man comes, will He find faith on the earth?"

We all have the option to quit when things are difficult. Quitting will not benefit you one single thing. It takes tenacity to keep going after what you believe until you get the right outcome. At times you may have to dig in your heels and refuse any attempts of the enemy to stop you. This nameless widow illustrates my point. Remember this, when God omits a name in the Bible, as with this nameless woman, you can plug your name into the story, take the lessons, and apply them to your life.

Jesus begins by sharing a parable with the disciples. What are parables? Often when Jesus spoke, He told short stories to illustrate a moral or religious principle. These short stories are called parables and He told approximately forty-six of them. He used parables/stories to connect with peoples' hearts. They always contained deep spiritual truths that had profound spiritual applications for the listeners. Jesus used the parable of the unjust judge to deliver some truths both to the disciples and to us. What you find in this story are some nuggets to help you stand until you get the victory. You should always pray, and never give up. Your answers and breakthroughs usually come from the most unlikely places and people.

The judge was earthly, cynical, merciless, unhelpful, and without principles. He did not care about the widow's concerns, nor did he treat her with neighborly love, as we are told to do in Mark 12:30-31. We are to love God with all our hearts and to love our neighbors as ourselves. In addition to not being concerned about the widow, he had no reverence for

God. He did not care that his injustice to her was a fight God would take up and win. He cared little for the widow's opinion of him; however, he could not withstand her persistence.

The widow was being harassed by her adversary. I would venture to say her adversary was possibly a debt collector. Since she was a widow, she had no one to care for her needs, but God is always protective of widows and orphans. There are many Scriptures in the Bible where we are told to take care of them. Yet, this judge refused to help her. We are told she did not go to the judge only once or twice; she went continually.

At first, the judge refused to help her. He did not care about her complaints and did not want to get involved with her struggles; even though it was his job to give her justice. Nonetheless, his unaccommodating attitude could not stop her from pursuing what was rightfully hers. She understood her rights and knew she deserved justice. It did not matter how long it took, she did not give up until she received her justice. This is also how you must be as it relates to those who are trying to hinder you from getting all God has for you. You must not get weary and give up but outlast them in the struggles.

Each time the judge saw the widow approaching his bench he probably thought, oh no, here she comes again! Can you imagine how irritated he must have felt as she continually went before him? The widow did not concern herself with whether she was bothering or wearing the judge out or not. She did, however, recognize he was attempting to wear her out with his continuous refusal to give her justice. Her focus was on the end result and that was to win over her adversary. She refused to quit; she refused to be intimidated by the judge;

she refused to allow the enemy to win, and she refused to give up.

The only way the enemy can ultimately win over you is if you allow him to wear you out and outlast you in your struggles. He cannot win when you refuse to give up. Remember, Jesus has already defeated him and given you the authority to stand your ground against him until you win. Like this widow, you have to persist until every obstacle that is in your path is overcome. If you must trample down the obstacles, or leap over them, then do it. Do not give the devil the satisfaction of having the last word in your life.

I have a friend, Rhonda, who has overcome some serious obstacles in her life, and recently she faced another one, but she faced it bravely. She went to the doctor for her yearly physical and received a call that there were some abnormalities in her results, so they arranged for an ultrasound. What is amazing about this testimony is Rhonda would have been very anxious and stressed before this ultrasound because this is how she would typically handle difficult situations.

Because of the transforming work God had done in her life, in previous years, she was not anxious or worried at all. She chose to only share these results with a few friends whom she knew would pray for her. She was confident and assured the doctors would not find any cancer in her body, and she did not move from her position of faith. She praised, worshiped, read her Bible, and then declared its life-giving words over herself. The night before the tests, she slept like a baby without any anxious moments. To hear her tell her story is an amazing testimony of what God has done to transform her from an anxious person to one who was peaceful during the storm. How did God transform her? Through the power of prayer, worship, and His Word.

It is evident God had succeeded in eradicating anxiety from her heart. She arrived for her test, and while there she comforted and encouraged others who had also received negative reports. She went through her exam in absolute peace, and when the result came, she already knew what it would be—no cancer. She did not need her earthly physician to give her this report, since God, the Great Physician, had already spoken clearly that all was well in her body.

Let's be honest here. Some of us would have been anxious and even fearful, but Rhonda recognized something we must all recognize—God will give us justice in the face of all the attacks of the enemy. He will not let the enemy have the last word or ultimate victory in our lives. We must be like Rhonda, fiercely holding on to our peace and hope in God until He transforms our lives. When we believe Him more, we will know we can trust Him even when things seem impossible in the natural.

Though the enemy desires to destroy you, God will give you justice over him—he will not succeed. Just like the unjust judge who refused justice to the widow for a time, the devil will yield to God and release his grip on you. As you keep standing against him using the Word of God, prayer, and worship as your weapons, he will have no recourse but to submit to God's authority. Using your voice to declare God's truths over your life will stop the enemy's constant harassment/assaults.

~

You Win

Although the judge held out for a while against the widow, he had to submit and give way to her wishes. His concern that she would never stop coming to him to receive justice until she prevailed, caused the judge to act. He granted her justice only because he thought about himself. She had worn him down. His justice was not because he knew she was right and she had a right to be vindicated, but because he recognized the determination in the widow. She stood her ground and was not going to allow her adversary to bully her and win. She refused to allow the judge to stop her from gaining her freedom from the continual harassment of her enemy. It was better to harass the judge than to be harassed herself. She recognized her adversary was not going to give up, so she did not give up. You and I must recognize the tactics of our enemy, the devil. Understand he wants to keep you from your victories. Refuse to be bullied.

Our adversary, the devil, never gives up. Listen to what the scripture tells us about him:

Be sober, be vigilant; because your adversary the devil, as a roaring lion, walketh about, seeking whom he may devour. Whom resist steadfast in the faith, knowing that the same afflictions are accomplished in your brethren that are in the world.

1 Peter 5:8-9 (KJV)

To be sober speaks of being alert and not becoming intoxicated. It is to be earnestly thoughtful, to be unhurried, calm, and to operate in moderation. Vigilant means to keep careful watch for danger or difficulties. It also means to be observant, attentive, alert, and eagle-eyed, while on the lookout for danger. The scriptures tell us we must be watchful, so the devil does not destroy us. We must not allow him to intoxicate us with the things of the world designed to destroy us. We are also warned to keep a watchful eye for the pitfalls of the enemy and to not relax our attention. When we are not focused or prayerful, this is when the enemy comes in and causes danger and difficulties in our lives.

To be eagle-eyed means to always be watchful. Let's look at how eagles see. The eagle is considered among the strongest in the animal kingdom. Their sight is estimated to be four to eight times stronger than that of the average human. An eagle may be able to spot a rabbit at 3.2km (about two miles) away. Although an eagle weighs approximately ten pounds, its eyes are the same size as those of a human.

As the eagle descends from the sky to attack its prey, the muscles in the eyes continuously adjust the curvature of its eyeballs to maintain sharp focus and accurate perception as they approach and attack. They have extraordinary vision which enables them to easily catch their prey. Their eyes may be larger than the size of their brains, and their color is the most prominent feature of their eyes because it allows them to see with crystal clarity. This is the reason people who have clear vision and can see well are often referred to as having eagle eyes.

If we as human beings had eagle vision, it is estimated we would see, with clarity, an ant crawling on the ground from the roof of a ten-story building. Everything in our sight would appear magnified and would be brilliantly colored. The eagle can see four to five times farther than the average human. Here is one last thing about the eagle that will help us as we pursue our victory: when a storm is approaching all other birds seek some type of shelter. The eagle, however, is the only known bird that avoids the storm not by hiding from it or cowering because of it, but by flying over it. It rises above the storm where it has a clearer vision of what is ahead. In the storms you are facing, remember above the clouds and the storms, the SON is still shining. He will give you victory over every storm.

Based on the above analogy, what does the Lord want us to do as it relates to frustrating the attacks of the enemy? We are to be alert and to watch continually for Him. Eagles swivel their heads continuously looking for prey. In the same way, we must constantly be looking around, ever aware of the enemy's plots and schemes, thus being ready to deal with any unexpected attacks. Since eagles are always alert, we must be vigilant—watchful, listening, praying, and being aware of what we could encounter. This means we cannot be lax or undisciplined in our walk of faith, but we have to be solid in our commitment to Jesus and steadfast as we pursue the plans He has for us. Understand this—the devil never gives up. He may leave you for a season, but he will return to continue his attacks because his goal is to annihilate you. This is what he tried to do with Jesus in the wilderness.

Luke 4:1-13 tells us Jesus was in the wilderness being tempted by the devil, and when he did not prevail, it says the devil left Jesus for a season. This meant he would return later to continue his attacks and deception.

The devil then returned to the Garden of Gethsemane just before the cross and caused Jesus to experience intense emotional pain and struggles. He was also present when the Jewish leaders attacked Jesus, flogged Him thirty-nine times, and then nailed Him to the cross. If he only left Jesus for a season, you can be assured he will only leave you until a more opportune time.

Be like the eagle. Stay aware and alert. Remember although the devil is not the real lion, he prowls around acting as if he is. There is only one real lion, and He is the Lion of the tribe of Judah, Jesus. He has eagle vision and is watching over you each day.

The widow gained victory over the enemy because she refused to give up. She had clear insight God would give her victory and could see above the storm because she tapped into the Father's vision for her life. The widow wore out her adversary and the judge with her persistence. You must do the same to prevail. Keep praying. Keep seeking after God. Keep hoping. Keep believing and trusting. Keep giving and continue going back to Jesus until you WIN.

God is not like the unjust judge; He is a just God who loves you. Using this story, Jesus showed us the contrast between God and man. What He wants you to understand is this—if this unjust judge finally yielded to this widow's demands, God who loves you will hear your cries for help. He finds great joy in answering you even when the answers are not immediate. He will give you justice, so don't stop praying or pursuing what is rightfully yours. Psalm 34:17 tells us God will answer us when we cry out to Him. I am crying out; how about you? Matthew 7:7-8 says, *"Ask and it will be given to you, seek and you shall find, knock and the door will be opened to you, for everyone who asks receives, he who seeks finds, and to him who knocks, the door will open."* Keep at it until you prevail.

A short while ago I was watching the news and saw this amazing story that reminded me of this widow. A Kenyan lady was running in a marathon and she was leading the pack of female runners. Just before the finish line, with victory in sight, exhaustion set in, and a short distance from the finish line she fell down. But the determined woman was not ready to quit. She began crawling on all fours, her eyes locked on the finish line. It was painful to watch her struggles. Her hands and knees were bloody, and tears were streaming down her face. Race volunteers rushed to her side with a wheelchair, but she refused to sit in it.

The determined woman continued inching forward down the track under the watchful eyes of the medical staff. As the crowd watched her determination and her perseverance, they stood up and began to cheer loudly. They were not cheering for the women who had taken the first or second place prizes, they were cheering for this woman, who with dogged determination and perseverance, was on her hands and knees crawling to the finish line. The runner who was in second place, far behind her, passed her and came in first; and the runner who was in third place, way behind her, also ran past her and came in second, but she kept crawling. The crowd encouraged her by shouting and applauding loudly as they saw her determination and perseverance under such severe difficulties. She came in third in the race and won the hearts of the people who watched her.

Trust me, those people did not remember the names of the first and second-place winners, but they remembered the name of this woman who showed them how to persevere through difficulties. The officials awarded her the same amount of money as the second-place winner. When asked why she did not quit, she said she did not start the race to not finish it.

You did not begin your race not to finish it. Life will knock you down at times, but you cannot afford to stay down. You must get up and keep persevering if you ever hope to win. During all the heartaches and pains that have overwhelmed you, God will give you justice. Do not allow the difficulties or the trials of life to disqualify you from finishing your race. Your goal is to cross the finish line and run into the bosom of the Savior.

Philippians 1:6 says, "Being confident of this very thing, that He who has begun a good work in you will complete it until the day of Jesus Christ." Jesus will finish the amazing work He started in you. Don't give up on God—He will never give up on you. You will prevail. You will win in the end. You will have a testimony of God's faithfulness in the struggles of life.

Remember, God is a just Judge and He is on your side.

You will WIN, and just like the widow woman, you can TRUST Him.

How Desperate Are You?

~

There are circumstances in life that, at times, can cause us to feel desperate. Have you ever experienced times of desperation? Did you feel as if you were not going to overcome it, or even make it through? Who did you turn to during these desperate times? Where did you find refuge from the storms? How desperate were you for God to break into your life and deliver you? As you answer these questions, remember you are not alone. Many people have felt the grip of desperation. The key to your freedom during these seasons is to remember Jesus and to anchor your hope in Him.

Psalm 56:3-4 says, *"When I am afraid, I will trust in you. In God, whose word I praise, in God I trust; I will not be afraid. What can mere mortals do to me?"*

David, who wrote this psalm, sought after God in his seasons of desperation. As he was pursued and slandered, he asked God to be merciful to him. I invite you to ask God to remember you as you face desperation.

The reasons we might feel desperate are varied —a health scare, the death of a loved one, the loss of a job, the fear of unwelcome news, or a feeling of hopelessness that seems permanent. Desperation means a loss of hope, surrender to despair, disappointment, cheerlessness, joylessness, and lose heart. Some of us have experienced any number of these things. Even as I write this book, I am reminded of what a difficult year this has been, not only in my life but in the lives of many people whom I love and pray for regularly. We have had to link our hearts in prayer and petition to Jesus, the only One who could help us. Psalm 112:7 tells us we do not need to fear bad news. Why? By remembering Jesus has conquered death, hell, and the grave, He has given us victory over them.

Early this year a dear friend, Kisun, was in our office assisting us with preparation for an upcoming mission trip. She had joined us just as we were beginning our daily prayer time, before starting the workday. I asked her to pray for us as we closed out. She asked if she could sing a song that had been in her heart all morning. She sang, "Turn Your Eyes Upon Jesus," written by Helen Howarth Lemmel. One line of the song says, "And the things of the earth will grow strangely dim in the light of His glory and grace." The song stayed in my heart the whole day as I prepared a message for the funeral. Kisun and the others laughed and talked the entire time they worked. Their joy and laughter were contagious, and I wished I could have joined them instead of preparing the message. Upon leaving our office, Kisun hugged me and laughingly said she was sorry they had made so much noise. I told her she was not sorry, and we both broke out into laughter. She was so joyful as she left our office.

Imagine my shock when, in the early hours of the next morning, I received a text saying she was being rushed to the hospital because of a brain aneurysm. Those of us who loved her began to pray with quiet desperation. As the difficult updates came in, I began to plead desperately for God to rescue and heal her. Throughout this desperate journey, my prayers were intense and heartfelt because I so wanted God to intervene and save her life. At one time during this sickness, she was recovering, and then, unexpectedly, she went home to be with the Lord. I had a hard time receiving and believing the news of her death, which was so unexpected after all the prayers we prayed. At her funeral, I was able to share with her family and friends the events of the previous day when she had worked in our office. I shared the joy, fun, and laughter she had with our staff and the other volunteers. I also shared with them the song that was in her heart that morning during our prayer time. As I concluded, I acknowledged she was indeed staring into the face of her Savior just as she had sung.

Her husband told me later that just before her death, she was praying for me and our ministries. What a surprise as well as a comfort to know she was thinking of us as she transitioned into heaven. I must admit my prayers for her were filled with heartfelt cries for God to spare her life. It was difficult to process she still went home to Jesus after her family, friends, and church members labored in prayer, during the entire time of her sickness. Listen: when we pray desperately and do not get the outcome we seek, this does not mean God has not heard us. It simply means God's purpose in the situation prevailed over our desires. As we wept over our loss, we were reminded God is all-knowing, and He is with us even through seasons of grief. He grieved with us. Read this poem that Rosalinda Garza, a member of one of our churches, shared with me. It will encourage you.

Tears

We will shed tears. They represent the cruelty we face, the agony we sustain, and the happiness we have no words to express. They are a symbol, a helpless cry to those around us.

To those we love and those we have yet to love. Tears do not physically hurt yet they can shatter all emotions, relieve the hidden tension, and enhance the cry for outrage. They are needed to show those around us we can feel. That life is a long, hard battle; we are human. Tears are hope. It provides us with knowledge and helps us learn from our mistakes. Enables us to overcome the tragedies we face. It remains a constant reminder to show what we need in our lifetime—to express a desire for comfort, understanding, and love.

Unfortunately, there will be seasons in your life when you will experience desperation and weep over your losses. Even when you do not get the outcome you hope for, you can still anchor your trust in God. God will see you through. He provides comfort during storms. He will carry you through each difficult season. Don't allow the feelings of desperation to overwhelm you to the point you take your focus off the One, Jesus Christ, who can help you. There are also seasons when you will weep for joy because something wonderful has happened in your life. Through all of this, as with Hannah in the Bible, God can turn your desperation into reasons to rejoice. Come with me as we discover how God blessed Hannah with a son, Samuel, for whom she desperately prayed.

A Cry from Deep within her Heart

Whenever the day came for Elkanah to sacrifice, he would give portions of the meat to his wife Peninnah and to all her sons and daughters. But to Hannah he gave a double portion because he loved her, and the Lord had closed her womb. And because the Lord had closed her womb, her rival kept provoking her in order to irritate her. This went on year after year. Whenever Hannah went up to the house of the Lord, her rival provoked her till she wept and would not eat. Elkanah her husband would say to her, "Hannah, why are you weeping? Why don't you eat? Why are you downhearted? Don't I mean more to you than ten sons?" Once when they had finished eating and drinking in Shiloh, Hannah stood up.

Now Eli the priest was sitting on a chair by the doorpost of the Lord's temple. In bitterness of soul Hannah wept much and prayed to the Lord. And she made a vow, saying, "O Lord Almighty, if you will only look upon your servant's misery and remember me, and not forget your servant but give her a son, then I will give him to the Lord all the days of his life, and no razor will ever be used on his head." As she kept on praying to the Lord, Eli observed her mouth. Hannah was praying in her heart, and her lips were moving but her voice was not heard. Eli thought she was drunk and said to her, "How long will you keep on getting drunk? Get rid of your wine." "Not so my lord," Hannah replied, "I am a woman who is deeply troubled. I have not been drinking wine or beer; I was pouring out my soul to the Lord. Do not take your servant for a wicked woman; I have been praying out of great anguish and grief." Eli answered "Go in peace and may the God of Israel grant you what you have asked of him."

1 Samuel 1:4-17 (NIV)

In this story of Hannah, you will find reasons to rejoice and to know God can give you a turn-around in your situation. Hannah was the primary wife of Elkanah. Her name means, "Grace of God, or God has favored me." Yet, as you study her life, you will see in the beginning she did not appear to be favored at all nor was she experiencing the grace God had extended to other women in her century. She was barren and appeared to have accepted this plight without a fight. God would not leave her in this condition; however, because He had a son for her, Samuel, whom He had chosen for His purpose.

God does not look favorably on us when we settle for less than what He proposes and has mapped out for our lives. He does not want us to become apathetic or comfortable in the conditions in which we find ourselves. We are told in Psalm 16:11 He does not want us to be satisfied with a mediocre life; not experiencing His fullness of life and joy. He wants us to prosper and to be healthy even as our souls prosper (3 John 1:2). This was His desire for Hannah, and today, this is His desire for you.

Elkanah also had a second wife, Peninnah, and she bore him many children while the love of his life struggled to bear one. Year after year, Peninnah taunted and provoked Hannah constantly about her barrenness. She would even provoke her when they went to the house of the Lord to worship and present their sacrifices. The enemy does not rest in his attacks on us. He dares to take his attacks even into our places of worship because he wants to break our focus and keep us from fellowship with God.

I have concluded that of all the other women Elkanah could have married, Peninnah did not end up in Hannah's house by accident but by divine design. God allowed an enemy to be planted in her house, so she would be provoked right into her destiny. This provocation pushed Hannah into depression, and desperation, and, into the presence of God where she began to seek Him earnestly in prayer.

Hannah was provoked on purpose because God had set the stage to birth destiny through her. Think about your life. Think of the many times you do not pray as you should until you are in the midst of difficulties. Many of us have not prayed as we should until we face trials. God knew allowing a second wife into this house would push Hannah out of compliance and into action. Destiny was in her womb and had to be birthed. At times God will use the enemy, our families, and even our friends to provoke us enough, to birth purpose in our lives. They will irritate us to such a degree we just have to do something about the irritation.

As was their yearly custom, Elkanah would take the family to the temple to offer their sin sacrifice, and he would give Hannah a double portion because of his great love for her. One day after being taunted and provoked, desperation drove Hannah into the presence of God. Desperation will drive us to the feet of the One who has the answers for our lives. Hannah felt hopeless and while weeping profusely, she finally did what God needed her to do—pray.

What situation pushes you to prayer? Have you ever wondered why we wait until we are in desperate situations before praying? I think this is because we may feel we can solve these problems on our own, so we don't seek God in the initial phase. Because of her deep need, Hannah made a rash promise, a vow. She would give her son back to the Lord all the days of his life. This was God's plan all along. God marked her son for His purpose. He allowed her desperation to drive her not only to prayer but into a covenant relationship with Him.

There are things God allows to happen to us (He is not the author of these difficulties) because out of them, greatness can be birthed in and through us. Think for a moment about some of the difficult struggles you have faced in life. What was borne in you? What have you borne out of those struggles? Did the struggles in any way diminish who you are or, did they advance you? If you did not advance, then this means you did not allow what the enemy used to harm you, to produce God's finest moments in your life.

I have said this to you before, but it bears repeating, God does not waste a single thing that happens in your life. He will take both the good and the bad and use them as stepping stones for your greatness and His glory. He will never allow the enemy to have the last say in the lives of any of His children.

When Eli saw Hannah praying, he thought she was drunk. Why? She was mouthing her prayer but no sounds were coming out of her mouth. Why was she praying silently? Because of Numbers 30! Let's look at the scripture:

If a woman living with her husband makes a vow or obligates herself by a pledge under oath and her husband hears about it but says nothing to her and does not forbid her, then all her vows or the pledges by which she obligated herself will stand. But if her husband nullifies them when he hears about them, then none of the vows or pledges that came from her lips will stand. Her husband has nullified them, and the Lord will release her. Her husband may confirm or nullify any vow she makes or any sworn pledge to deny herself. But if her husband says nothing to her about it from day to day, then he confirms all her vows or the pledges binding on her. He confirms them by saying nothing to her when he hears about them. If, however, he nullifies them some time after he hears about them, then he is responsible for her guilt.

From this scripture, we see God had placed a limitation on Hannah's vow as a woman. Therefore, her husband could nullify the vow if he did not agree with it. Hannah is praying silently to ensure that nobody, not even the priest, could hear her heartfelt petition or vow to God. She was taking no chances that anyone might cancel her vow. She knew her husband could nullify it because of the husband's ownership of the woman's property in marriage, including her children. She is making a courageous move in treating her future child and her vow as her own, between her and the Lord alone. Once she explained to Eli the priest, that she was not drunk but pouring out her sorrows to God, he blessed her and prophesied God would grant her the desires of her heart. God heard the prophet and honored His word to Hannah. She conceived and gave birth. She named her son, Samuel, meaning, "Because I asked the Lord for him."

Hannah told her husband later about the vow and he agreed she could give her son to the Lord. Remember, he loved her and would do whatever she wanted to ensure her happiness. God knew Elkanah's heart and knew he would consent to His plan and his wife's vow. Elkanah could have nullified her vow and given a guilty offering for breaking it, but he did not. Let me ask. What can desperation birth out of your heart? The reason I am in ministry today is because of a heartfelt cry to God to not allow me to live a mediocre life. There was more to my life than just existing from day to day. I was desperate for something more. I still live in a place of desperation, declaring often—more of Jesus and less of me. At times I say—all of Jesus and none of me. I am in relentless pursuit of Jesus, so I can become more like Him each day. How about you?

Promise Received/Promise Kept

Hannah received her promised son.

> *Early the next morning they arose and worshipped before the Lord and then went back to their home at Ramah. Elkanah lay with Hannah his wife, and the Lord remembered her. So in the course of time Hannah conceived and gave birth to a son. She named him Samuel, saying, "Because I asked the Lord for Him."*
>
> *1 Samuel 1:19:22 (NIV)*

God answered Hannah's desperate plea because He intended to use Samuel to govern and judge His people. Hannah, however, had no prior insight into God's amazing plan for Samuel, so she cooperated with Him unknowingly and kept the baby at home until he was weaned. In Hannah's century, children who were dedicated had to be at least a month old because of the high infant mortality rate. A child was weaned around three years old; at that age, it was likely to survive to adulthood. Hannah did not deliver her son to God when he was only a month old but waited until he was much older. What I want you to see is this—Hannah's heart was as pure as her promise to give her son to God. She wanted to give God her absolute best—a healthy, vibrant, strong child to serve wholeheartedly before Him. Not only was she willing to give up her only child, but her sacrifice speaks of a desire to please the One who had lifted her out of shame and depression.

Her faith was pure and so was her sacrifice. She made sure her sacrifice would be a perfect one—a healthy child. This is important because whenever the Israelites were to sacrifice an animal to God, it had to be clean, without spot or blemish, and not diseased. Hannah was desperate to conceive a son and took careful measures to do so. She was just as careful in her presentation of him to God.

Consider this with me and assess what you would do if you were in Hannah's place. As she nursed her son, she knew someone else would take care of his needs as he grew into manhood. When the day arrived for her to deliver on her promise, I am sure she was sad, but she kept her word. In Leviticus 5:4-6, God had made provisions for redeeming vows or pledges in money. Hannah could have chosen not to honor her promise if she simply could not part with her son. Honoring her word was self-sacrifice and speaks of her devotion to God. Ecclesiastes 5:5 says, "*It is better not to vow than to make a vow and not fulfill it.*"

Hannah gave up her greatest desire for God's ultimate desire. She packed up her son's clothes, went to the temple, and there delivered her only child to Eli, the priest. She was not sad or pitiful when she delivered him; she worshipped God. She sang a powerful song as an indication of a heart that was open and ready to serve God in any way He chose because He had helped her.

As I look at her song and prayer, I am reminded of Mary, who in Luke 1 also rejoiced that God had chosen her, a lowly maiden, and given her the privilege of being the mother of Jesus. Hannah completed her vow the way she had begun it— she prayed. God had kept His promise to her, and she now had the privilege of honoring her promise to Him. Listen: she would only see him once a year when they made the journey for the yearly sacrifice. She had no other children at home to find consolation in; yet, she walked away from the temple with her empty arms. Hannah's heart was full of gratitude to God for keeping His promise to her and lifting her from shame and pain. Now, let me ask you, what would you have done?

This was a woman who was desperate to see God's plans unfold in the earth, although she did not fully understand all her son would become. God had planned a great destiny for Samuel and had to get Hannah's heart prepared so she would readily release him. This was accomplished through barrenness and a long season of waiting. Do you see it? In our struggles, God can do amazing things in our lives. He birthed something wonderful through Hannah even when she despaired of ever producing an heir for Elkanah. In your struggles, God is preparing a greater destiny and a future filled with hope, prosperity, and promotion, for you.

~

Blessed Beyond Measure

Have you discovered yet that God is kind and compassionate? He never forgets our sacrifices. You cannot out-give Him. Hannah discovered this. As Samuel grew, God was with him. Eventually, Eli died and Samuel took his place. Think carefully as I rehearse and summarize what God did for her. For years Hannah was mocked, scorned, taunted, and provoked. She was looked down on for her barrenness and was considered cursed by God. With a sense of hopelessness, she prayed to God, and He answered her at the right time. He then used her longed-for son to be the prophet of the Israeli people, the man who spoke to and heard from God personally. This is how God rewards us for our sacrifices when we willingly say yes to His plans.

Each time Hannah, Peninnah (Hannah's enemy), Elkanah, Peninnah's children, the Israelites, and those who may have thought Hannah was cursed, went to the temple to present their sacrifices, there they saw Samuel, a prophet in training, and the son of the once barren Hannah. God did not give her just any son. He gave her one who was chosen, anointed, and throughout history was known as one of the purest, most noble men who ever lived. He gave her a son who became famous as one of God's greatest prophets—His mouthpiece.

Each time the people heard the name Samuel, they could not help but remember and reflect on who birthed him—Hannah. Consider this—all the other mothers who had children during Hannah's century, their children passed from history without a mention, but not Hannah's son. Centuries later we are still hearing and learning about the once barren woman's son. *God keeps His promises.* Engrave those words on your heart because He will keep His promises to you as well.

The Bible tells us that year by year Hannah made coats and took them to Samuel. Eli would bless Elkanah and Hannah and say, "The Lord give you descendants from this woman for the loan that was given to the Lord", and God answered. He gave her three additional sons and two daughters. Five children altogether. The number five means grace and favor. I told you at the beginning of the chapter Hannah's name meant, "Grace or God has favored me." God fulfilled the meaning of her name with these five children. Throughout her life, when people called her name, they were calling her destiny into fruition. God indeed graced her and poured His abundant favor into her life. He provoked destiny out of her. He wants to provoke you into prayer which will lead you to the feet of Jesus, to seek Him for His great plans for your future.

I close with a few questions for you. What is causing your distress? Could it have been sent to provoke you into your purpose? Could it push you into the destiny for which you were born? When you are being provoked by the enemy, and feelings of desperation and depression are trying to set in, pray to Jesus. He will birth vision and greatness in your life.

Remember, your desperation can release you into a future filled with hope and blessings.

Just like Hannah, you can TRUST Him.

NOT FORSAKEN

~

Years ago, there was a song that talked about not being forgotten. The words reminded me even when people are not mindful of us, God is always for us. He never leaves nor forsakes us. People can and will overlook us at times, but God knows us intimately. From Genesis to Revelation, we find God has never forsaken His people, even when repeatedly they strayed from Him. The Israelites fell into continual sin and it drove them away from God. Yet, God was always right where they left Him, ready and willing to receive them when they repented and returned to Him.

Have you ever wondered why God does not simply give up on us when we constantly sin and disobey Him? The answer is simple—He loves us. When He created Adam and Eve, He was creating a family for Himself. He wanted fellowship with people who had their own will and could make their own choices. He did not create people who would be forced to obey and serve Him, but those who would choose obedience because they reciprocated His love. You and I each have our own free will. We are not obligated to develop a relationship with God; we get to choose Him over our own desires. We decide if we want to accept the sacrifice of His Son, Jesus. By an act of our will, we say YES to Jesus, and YES to God's plans for our lives and futures.

God put Adam in the Garden of Eden with only one instruction—you are free to eat from any tree in the garden, but you must not eat from the tree of the knowledge of good and evil, for when you eat of it you will surely die (Genesis 2:15-17).

This was Adam's opportunity to choose God over his own desires. This was a test to see if he loved God more than himself. Consider that he and God had an intimate fellowship for a significant amount of time, time enough to name all the animals and do all he accomplished before God gave Eve to him. Yet, when the test to prove His love and devotion came, and even with the threat of death, He still chose sin and his own will over God. He abandoned God, but God did not forsake him.

When the woman saw that the fruit of the tree was good for food and pleasing to the eye, and also desirable for gaining wisdom, she took some and ate it. She also gave some to her husband, who was with her, and he ate it.

Genesis 3:6 (NIV)

Even after Adam and Eve sinned and damaged their relationship with Him, God came down from Heaven to see about them because He knew without His help, they could not survive in the new world their sin had created. They were naked and did not know how to clothe themselves. The animals Adam had once named and lived peacefully with were now at war with each other. Some of these animals could potentially harm or kill them. God did not forsake them even though a holy God cannot be in the presence of sin. He came one final time to rescue, prepare, and equip them for the future they had created for themselves. It was a future filled with pain and sorrow. It was only when they experienced this that were they able to comprehend the meaning of death—complete separation from God. No more intimate talks in the garden, and no more time basking in the presence of God, their Father. They had abandoned God and destroyed the family unit He had created with them.

Think about stories you have either heard, seen on television, or read, about people who were forsaken. How did you feel when you heard these stories? Usually, these people will say no one wanted them and they had been abandoned. They felt discarded and rejected. They were cast aside. Somebody had deserted, left them rejected, and desolate. This is what it means to be forsaken. If you have ever had any of these experiences, then you know the feelings of hopelessness that come along with them. What you can be assured of is this—Jesus will never forsake you.

Isaiah 49:15-16 tells us this, *"Can a mother forget the baby at her breast and have no compassion on the child she has borne?*

Though she may forget, I will not forget you! See, I have engraved you on the palms of my hands; your walls are ever before me." God cannot forget or forsake you because you are permanently engraved on the palms of His hands. Think about the significance of that statement—He engraved you where He took the nail prints for your freedom and salvation. When you feel forsaken, rejected, neglected, or abandoned, the enemy is trying to undermine your value and status with God. He is attempting to steal your confidence in who God says you are—dearly loved. Don't let him get the victory; claim your position as a son or daughter of God.

On one of our mission trips to San Salvador, while we were ministering in an extremely poor village, we came across seven children aged two to twelve who were living alone because their parents were in jail on drug charges. An aunt came to take charge of them for a brief period, but she also had problems with drugs and was soon arrested. These children were barely surviving, eating fruits from trees in their neighborhood. They were abandoned, malnourished, unclean, and unkempt. When we approached the gate to their home, the eldest child quickly locked the gate because she thought we were the authorities coming to take them away.

The pastors who took us into the community knew them and would stop by to provide what little assistance they could. After recognizing the pastors, they let us in. Because they were so malnourished, the eldest girl who was twelve looked like she was eight or nine years old. Their clothes were piled high on the veranda because she could not wash them. I must tell you we have been to many nations before and since this one, but I have never seen children in the shocking condition that these were in. I could not contain my tears.

Seeing a strange vehicle outside the home, one of the neighbors and her children stopped by to see what was happening. I asked how it was the children were in such a desperate condition with neighbors all around them. She said various neighbors tried to provide food but since most of them were living in poverty, they could not provide much and still take care of their own families. We asked the neighbor to bring water and bathe them while we hunted through our bags of clothing for items that would fit. The two-year-old girl wore a raggedy t-shirt without any undergarments and was severely bitten by bugs. Remembering I had seen a pizza restaurant on our way into the community, I sent one of the pastors back to town to buy pizza and drinks to feed them. The next day we went grocery shopping and bought enough food to feed them for a month. We partnered with one of the churches and hired a neighbor to take care of them until a family member could take over.

Two years later we returned and found out a twenty-one-year-old cousin and her new husband, had decided to take on the responsibility of caring for these seven kids. After finishing our event, I went into the community to see where they lived. It was a safe clean home, and they were clean, well fed, and prospering. The second oldest child stared at me for a while and finally, she said I know you; I said you do? She said yes, you are the lady who gave us pizza. When we first visited their home, it was extremely dark, so I was surprised she recognized me. We did many things for them in those two days but as you can see, what she remembered most was that we fed them because this was their greatest need.

Can you see the mercy of our God in the lives of these abandoned children? He sent a couple of strangers from another country into this community even though there were many others equally as poor. He caused the Pastor to make his last stop at this house, and in so doing rescued these desperate children. God is loving and merciful, He knows those who have been abandoned and will come to their aid. If you feel as if no one cares about you, let me say loudly and clearly, that our Savior cares deeply for you. He knows where you are, and He will send you help. He wants your joy in Him to be complete and overflowing.

~

Happiness versus Joy

It is reasonable to conclude many of us have experienced times of happiness, sorrow, and joy. We have enjoyed feelings of satisfaction and well-being during seasons when we were happy and content, but the problem with happiness is it is not long-lasting. It is an unstable emotion that does not endure but changes often. It is subjective—biased, one-sided, and slanted. We are temporarily happy when we acquire things—money, status, education, expensive houses, cars, and other fleeting things. The effects of happiness, however, are temporary because situations are temporary.

The things we acquire only give us a temporary fix before

we need something else to satisfy another need. Think about a time when you received a gift. The feelings of euphoria were high, but after a while the feelings waned and you set the gift aside, desiring something else. It is not what we get that produces lasting happiness or fulfillment, but when we give that causes fulfillment.

When we feel forsaken, these feelings rob us of our joy. They make us wonder if we have any support and cause us to question just how valuable we are to others. Because many of us depend on others to make us happy, we feel abandoned when they forsake or reject us. It is hard to comprehend why they would walk away from us. I only hope you have discovered that no person or thing can give you lasting happiness. Jesus is our only source of true happiness and joy.

Have you ever thought about the relationship between joy and happiness? There is a connection—we *all* experience them. Daily we get to choose whether we will be unhappy or joyful. I once heard someone say there is no un-joy, only unhappiness. What was he saying? We cannot undo joy, but we can undo our happiness depending on our emotional state. When we struggle with being forsaken, it's the enemy attempting to rob the joy of the Lord from our hearts. When we lose our joy, we lose our strength (Nehemiah 8:10). Without strength we are incapable of accomplishing anything of value with our lives and for God.

Joy is an attitude of the heart. It is thankfulness despite our circumstances and is an internal, long-lasting condition that does not depend on our emotions. Joy is a fruit of the Spirit and comes from deep within our spirit; from the Holy Spirit who is the one who fills us with this joy. So, to have continual joy, you must stay connected to the Holy Spirit. Amid being forsaken, you can still maintain your joy. Joy does not diminish your pain or elevate the feelings of being forsaken or abandoned, but it sustains you in it. Pain cannot eradicate your joy and likewise, joy cannot eradicate your pain; they often co-exist in the same space.

Amid the untimely death of my brother, there were moments when we laughed while thinking about him, and other moments when we wept. The joy was there while we endured the pain, and it sustained us during this difficult season. Deep abiding joy can thrive even while being forsaken. Joy comes from knowing God is with you, He is present in your struggles and has a purpose in your pain. Remember, in the book of Job, after he had gone through severe hardships, Job continually prayed to God as he tried to understand his pain. When God finally responded to Job in chapter thirty-eight of Job, verse one, *"He answered Job out of the storm."* He was in the storm, in the struggles with Job, and later gave him double for all the troubles he endured. Having and maintaining your joy means you are connecting to something greater than your emotions. Joy is a conscious decision you make to be peaceful and at rest no matter what you are facing. When we experience joy, it calms our souls.

Remember, the Bible records that for the joy that was set before Him, Jesus endured the cross (Hebrews 12:2). What was His joy? It was our salvation; our redemption; our freedom; and our reconnection with God, our Father. If Jesus had operated based on being happy about His suffering, He would not have made it to the cross. Nothing in His painful situation could have led Him to ultimate, long-lasting happiness, but joy was His constant companion. Joy helped Him endure the pain and suffering because the end results were worth it. His joy and pain co-existed together in the same space and kept Him pressing toward the ultimate sacrifice—His life given in exchange for ours.

So, let's examine the difference between joy and happiness. Joy lasts, happiness is temporary. Joy is internal, happiness is external. If you choose it, joy can remain with you through the storms, while happiness evades you in the storms. Joy brings lasting hope, while happiness brings temporary hope. Daily you choose which path you will take. Will you allow the joy of the Lord to steady you even when forsaken? Or will you allow the unstable emotions of happiness to rob you from experiencing contentment no matter what? The Apostle Paul tells us he learned how to be content in whatever situation he faced (Philippians 4:11-13). How? Because he anchored his hope, joy, and life in Jesus. Jesus was forsaken by the Jews, the disciples, the people in His hometown, and His family, but He stayed true to God. He did not allow their abandonment to keep Him from becoming our Savior. He held onto His joy and finished His course.

Now, Jesus is seated at the right hand of God enjoying His rewards. He knows you might have been forsaken by people, but He will never forsake you. He knows the enemy wants to steal your joy and peace, but He wants you to anchor your hope in Him. He will give you the victory and you will receive the rewards if you remain steady in your struggles. To remain steady—remember to lean heavily into Him, He will hold onto you and keep you safe.

∿

Sorrow Will Not Overtake Me

As I reflect on the many examples in the Bible of people who were forsaken by those close to them, I am reminded of Leah. Let's look together at her life and see God's faithfulness to her.

As soon as Laban heard the news about Jacob, his sister's son, he hurried to meet him. He embraced him and kissed him and brought him to his home, and there Jacob told him all these things. Then Laban said to him, "You are my own flesh and blood." After Jacob stayed with him for a whole month, Laban said to him, "Just because you are a relative of mine, should you work for me for nothing? Tell me what your wages should be. "Now Laban had two daughters; the name of the older was Leah, and the name of the younger was Rachel. Leah had weak eyes, but Rachel was lovely in form, and beautiful. Jacob was in love with Rachel and said, "I'll work for seven years in return for your younger daughter Rachel." Laban said, "It's better that I give her to you than to some other man. Stay here with me." So Jacob served seven years to get Rachel, but they seemed like only a few days to him because of his love for her. Then Jacob said to Laban, "Give me my wife. My time is completed, and I want to lie with her." So Laban brought together all the people of the place and gave a feast. But when evening came, he took his daughter Leah and gave her to Jacob, and Jacob lay with her.

Leah's name means weary, impatient, or faint. She experienced happiness, joy, and sorrow throughout her life. She was weary and impatient with all the difficulties she faced. We are introduced to her when Laban, Jacob's uncle, tricked him into marrying her. Jacob loved her sister, the beautiful Rachel, and had worked for her for seven years. On his wedding night, Laban, the trickster, gave him a substitute wife—Leah. His reason was the younger daughter should not be married before the older one. The Scripture describes Leah as having 'weak eyes', as she was apparently not beautiful to look at. Historians believe she was approximately fourteen years old when Jacob arrived. So, since Jacob worked seven years for Rachel, then Leah was approximately twenty-one years old when they married. This was considered old for that century when they usually married between thirteen and sixteen years old. Jacob was justifiably upset, but he later married Rachel after working another seven years for her while remaining married to Leah.

Surely Leah knew Jacob loved Rachel, so why marry him? She had no choice but to obey her father. During that century women did not have many rights and therefore she could not voice her opinion. It was the custom of the day to marry the older daughter first, and it is quite probable Leah loved Jacob, but she paid dearly for her part in the deception.

God, however, has this amazing ability to fight for those who are disadvantaged. He looked out for, and watched over the underdogs of that time, even as He still does today. You will find throughout the Bible God was mindful of the poor, widows, orphans, and the aliens that lived among the Israelites. If you are experiencing feelings of being forsaken or that you are not good enough, remember, that He is watching over you today. Jacob was tolerating his marriage to Leah, but God remembered her. While Rachel, the love of his life was barren,

God made Leah very fruitful, and she birthed many children. Rachel was envious of Leah and very demanding of Jacob. In Genesis 30:1-4 she told Jacob to give her children, or she would die—very dramatic. Jacob became angry and challenged her as to whether he was in God's place since it was God who was keeping her barren. Like Sarah, Abraham's wife, she became desperate for a child and gave her servant to Jacob to produce a son for her. Jacob slept with the servant and God caused her to conceive immediately, while Rachel was still struggling with barrenness. Do you see it? God deliberately kept her from conceiving. The problem was not Jacob's fertility but Rachel's barrenness. Why? Is it possible God was working on her heart, her character, and her love not only for Jacob but also for Leah and others? Nowhere in this story do you find any mention that Rachel loved Jacob.

Rachel and Leah had a challenging relationship, not unlike many sisters today. There was jealousy and competition between them. Rachel was beautiful to look at but Leah had something that transcended outer beauty. Someone said, there are two kinds of beauty—one God gives to some people at birth, and the other when He enters our hearts and transforms our lives from the inside out. Listen, no matter how unattractive we may think a person is, when God enters their life, His presence makes all the difference. His light, His glory, and His splendor will radiate from them and make them beautiful. God's special beauty will outlast any natural, earthly beauty that fades over time. Leah possessed the type of beauty that lasted throughout her life.

Leah's Steadfast Hope and Faith

Genesis 29:31 says *when the Lord saw Leah was not loved, he opened her womb, but Rachel was barren.* Question— did God not recognize Jacob loved Rachel not Leah?

Yes, He did. Is it possible God expected over a period of time Jacob's heart would change toward Leah, and he would develop a love for her? He probably did. When this did not happen, God acted. He gave Leah many children. Leah had six sons and one daughter and named her children as a reflection of her faith and steadfast hope in God. She named her firstborn son Reuben, which means 'Behold a son'; she had presented Jacob with an heir. Her second son was named Simeon, which means 'Hearing'; this was Leah's acknowledgment that God was indeed hearing her cry of being forsaken. She named her third son Levi, meaning 'Joined'. As you examine his name, you come away with the impression that through this son Leah hoped to be more closely joined to Jacob. She named her fourth son, Judah, meaning 'Praise'. Leah, it appears, was beginning to realize how good God had been to her and chose to praise Him.

Despite being forsaken and abandoned by her father and husband, God had been a very present help in her life. She discovered the greatest person in the universe was by her side and was fighting, rooting for her. With this son, Leah set all negative emotions, feelings of hopelessness, and any bitterness that may have lodged in her soul, aside. She began to praise God.

Leah named her fifth son, Issachar, which means 'Reward and Recompense.' She discovered how faithful God had been to her. The number five means grace. God's grace was flowing in great abundance towards her because she was unloved and forsaken. God was rewarding her for her steadfast hope and trust in Him. She named her sixth son, Zebulun, which means 'Prince'. Just thinking of this name points us to understanding she was discovering how valuable she was to God. She began to acknowledge her status as the daughter of a King.

Leah discovered even though others may have not placed a high value on who she was because of her looks or lack thereof, God saw her as precious and valuable and had never over-looked her. She discovered her self-worth and realized God had presented her with a precious gift. She said, "This time my husband will treat me with honor because I have borne him six sons." She was still hopeful her husband's heart would change and turn towards her.

God took someone who was forsaken and rejected both by her husband and sister and promoted her, restoring her hope and joy. Throughout all of this, Jacob still loved Rachel more. God gave Rachel a son through her servant, Bilhah, whom she named Dan meaning 'God has vindicated; He has listened to my plea and given me a son.' The servant conceived again, and Rachel named him Naphtali meaning, 'I have had a great struggle with my sister, and I have won'. Rachel was competing with a sister whom God had blessed abundantly.

Rachel, the beautiful sister, saw herself as less than Leah, the one who lacked outer beauty. Are you seeing how God works? He does not place a high value on what people think is most valuable. He places value on what He sees in our hearts and promotes us based on what He finds there, hence Leah's abundant blessings. When Leah stopped bearing children, she decided to compete with Rachel and gave Jacob her servant, Zilpah, to continue her lineage. She named this first son, Gad, which means, 'What good fortune'. The servant conceived and had a second son whom she named Asher, meaning 'How happy I am'.

Finally, the scripture says God remembered Rachel and gave her a son whom she named Joseph, meaning 'God has taken away my disgrace'. She then prayed God would give her another son, and He did.

Leaving the Place of Service

As Jacob left Laban's service, taking his wives and children, God blessed him abundantly. Upon leaving her father, Rachel took his household gods and put them inside her camel's saddle, and Laban came searching for them. Rachel was sitting on them and lied about what she had done. It's evident Rachel was not connected to the true God of the universe to have stolen some of her father's false gods who had no power at all to help her. It is also evident she had some character issues. Yet, God remembered Rachel and gave her another son, but she died in childbirth. While she was dying, she named her baby Ben-Oni, meaning son of pain. The name was an allusion to Rachel's dying just after she had given birth. Jacob, however, renamed him Benjamin which means son of my right hand. Jacob obviously understood the importance and impact of a name on a child's future and refused to allow his son to be called the son of pain throughout his life.

I said earlier in the chapter that although others may forsake you, God will never forsake you. He will stand by your side and give you favor. He will vindicate you and cause you to shine while others may overlook you. God will demonstrate He is for you and with you, and He will fight for you and win. He did this for Leah. Even though Jacob loved Rachel instead of Leah, and even though he loved Rachel's sons, Joseph, and Benjamin, more than Leah's children, God was still for Leah.

As Jacob prepared to meet Esau before Rachel's death, he began plotting how to save his life and the lives of his family. Once again, Leah discovered she was still not his first choice. Jacob placed Rachel and her children last in the long caravan he had formed to meet Esau, giving them a greater chance of escaping if Esau had not forgiven him and chose to destroy them instead. How hurtful that must have been to Leah to still be in second place in the eyes of her husband after the many children she had personally given him. But God...

Let's look at how God won the victory for Leah. It was Leah, not Rachel, who bore Judah through whose lineage our Savior Jesus came; and it was through Levi, another of Leah's sons, from whom the priestly line which personally ministered to God, was chosen. She had all six children before God gave Rachel her first son. Leah outlived Rachel and enjoyed a longer period of being married to Jacob than her sister. She was the first and last wife of Jacob. Leah, not Rachel was regarded as the mother of Israel for producing six of the twelve sons who made up the twelve tribes of Israel. Rachel only had two sons, and their two servants, Bilhah and Zilpah had two sons each. Through Leah's son, Judah, the great King David was born.

When Jacob was buried, he was buried next to Leah and not Rachel. God remembered Leah because she was unloved by man and forsaken, but He dearly loved her. God was with Leah throughout her difficult life, and He was her champion. He caused her to triumph over all her enemies and gave her a significant place in the Bible and history. God restored her joy and helped her banish any unhappiness by His constant presence in her life. He filled her with hope.

God is with you and restores your hope after you have been forsaken. He does not look the other way when you face difficulties and does not rejoice in injustice. He sees that people have forsaken you and left you wounded, and He comes to your rescue. God wipes away your hurts, heals your wounds, and gives you standing and position over all those who dare to overlook you. He will reward you when others dismiss you and will ensure you have a legacy that outlives others. Find your hope and joy in Him today.

Remember, God hears your cries, and He will never forsake you.

Just like Leah, you can TRUST Him.

GIVE ME MY MOUNTAIN

Have you ever considered the level of your faith and trust in God? Do you really believe He will do what He has promised you? What happens to your faith when you find yourself in a long waiting season? There are times when we feel strongly that our relationship with God is extremely solid; therefore, we do not do much self-examination. As a result, we may have drifted from His narrow path onto the broad path without being aware of it.

Matthew 7:13-14 tells us, *"Enter through the narrow gate. For wide is the gate and broad is the road that leads to destruction, and many enter through it. But small is the gate and narrow the road that leads to life, and only a few find it."*

Some of us struggle to believe in God at times because several things we have prayed for have not yet manifested. We are not entirely sure what the delay is, but we are aware He can give us a quicker outcome and are not sure why He has not. In these seasons we can get stuck. There are others though, who do not concern themselves about how long it takes God to move. They have absolute confidence He will, and nothing can shake their belief. Those with this level of faith have found throughout their journey with God that He can be trusted. They have found Him to be true to His Word and His promises. They have discovered He is faithful and cannot lie.

One of my favorite scriptures in the Bible is found in Numbers 23:19-20 – "Arise, Balak, and listen; hear me, son of Zippor. God is not a man, that he should lie, nor a son of man, that he should change his mind. Does he speak and then not act? Does he promise and not fulfill? I have received a command to bless, he has blessed, and I cannot change it." King Balak hired Balaam to curse the children of Israel because he was afraid of them. They were a massive group of people, and God fought for them and defeated all their enemies. God was fearsome in their midst, and this terrified the other nations. After seeing how severely God had dealt with the Israelites' enemies, King Balak and his people were terrified and sought help from Balaam.

God did not want Balaam to curse His children and told him this, yet he desired to go. He went at the command of King Balak and in disobedience to God. As a result, God sent an angel to kill him but his donkey saved his life. Each time Balaam opened his mouth to curse the children of Israel, only blessings came out. In Numbers 23:8 Balaam said, "How can I curse those whom God has not cursed? How can I denounce those whom the Lord has not denounced?" This made the king angry, and he demanded to know what Balaam was doing. Balaam said, "Must I not speak what the Lord puts in my mouth?" Even if Balaam wanted to curse the Israelites as the king desired him to do, it was impossible because God was against it. When God is fighting for you, the enemy will NEVER ultimately prevail against you. He may score a few points, but God will still cause you to be victorious in the end.

Every negative word, situation, or challenge you face is subject to God's approval. The enemy cannot slip anything detrimental into your life without God's knowledge. If God allows difficulties to enter your life, then know He sees how this will benefit you in the end. He uses adverse situations to grow your faith and showcase His power in your life. God never stages or brings the attacks against us, the enemy does. Some people blame God for the ills in their lives and the world. They feel He should put a stop to it. They have forgotten God has given man a "free will" and some choose to use that will to bring harm and destruction instead of good. Certainly, God could stop them but then He would be interfering in the very thing He gave us—free will. This is the ability to make our own choices. This does not mean God is not whispering truths into peoples' hearts before they commit atrocities. They simply choose not to hear and obey Him.

As you face difficulties, here is a promise from the Word of God for you: Isaiah 54:17, *"No weapon that is formed against you shall prosper; and every tongue that rises against you in judgment you shall condemn.*" It goes on to say 'this is your heritage because you are a servant of the Lord and your righteousness comes from Him.' When you face difficult and painful times, God is not distant. He is not only with you but is fighting for you. He has not left you to figure it out on your own. God is not an uncaring Father, but a Father who stays close to His children and is mindful of our needs and struggles. He has given us a way of outtrusting Him no matter how dire the situations might be. He will come through for you every time if you only trust Him. Listen to this story I heard and see how God wars on behalf of His children.

There was this poor widow whose husband left her and her children the house they had labored hard to build. Without her knowledge, her husband's relatives illegally sold her house. The widow refused to leave her home when the new owner came to evict her. The case went to court. When the judge asked who her lawyer was she told him Jesus Christ, her Savior, would stand up for her and be her defense because she could not afford an attorney. The case dragged on for twelve years, and during those years, Jesus indeed defended her. Her relatives and the new owner tried to use witchcraft against her and her family, but Jesus provided total protection and was in absolute control of the situation. He gave her favor as her case went before one judge after another. Finally, she went before the highest court in the land and Jesus continued to be her only defense. After many trials and struggles, He gave her divine favor and she was completely victorious.

She simply believed Jesus would help her, and because of her faith, He delivered her in great power from her oppressors.

This woman did not let go of her hope and confidence in God's ability to see her through the tough times. She anchored her faith in the One she knew had all the power and authority she needed to vindicate her. How about you? For what do you believe Jesus? Is it your family, relationships, spouse, health, finances, a business, a promotion, or a vision for your destiny? I can assure you Jesus will do it! He has all power and authority in His hands, and He alone can turn the hearts of people and give them justice.

Difficulties Won't Stop Me

Some of you have discovered the ploy of the enemy is to bring difficulties into your lives to stop you from receiving the blessings God has for you. Listen: though he cannot stop you, he can slow your momentum. His tactics can delay what God wants to accomplish in your life.

As you study the Bible, you will find many instances where the devil caused people to miss what God had for them. The devil will often use fear to cripple us and keep us from moving into our seasons of blessings. You must learn to recognize when he is at work in your midst. How? When God gives you a word, and you know God wants you to take steps towards its fulfillment but unexpected challenges arise, it's the enemy attempting to keep you from moving forward. You know he is attacking you when problems arise just before you begin the journey toward your next promotion or assignment. He used these tactics against the children of Israel throughout their journey to the Promised Land. Many of the Israelites did not get to enjoy the promised blessings of milk and honey because they did not circumvent these tactics. But before I share their story with you, let me share a personal example.

At the beginning of my ministry, I was invited to go on my first international ministry trip to Honduras to teach the Word of God. This would be the first time I had taught the message of God outside of the United States. What I did not know was that God would birth the mission component of the ministry during this trip. The ministry was only six months old, and the person who invited me paid the way for me and my Administrator to go. A couple of weeks before we traveled, my dad, who had always been healthy, was diagnosed with prostate cancer. Hearing this news was difficult and sent me into a season of prayer. I live in Houston and my parents live in Michigan. I was making plans to be with them for the surgery when I learned the date of the surgery. Guess when it was scheduled? The day I was traveling and also scheduled to minister at the first event in Honduras. I knew this was a distraction from the enemy, but it was also a test of my devotion to God. I realized this news did not take God by surprise, and therefore, I needed to decide if I would honor Him and keep my promise or cancel the trip at the last minute.

Some of you will find the next statement I make difficult to hear but stay with me. I called my parents and reminded them of my commitment, and they understood. I love them but since I was a child, I have loved God more. They were not surprised I chose to go to Honduras and minister. After we landed and arrived at the church, I called them and heard the report that the surgery went well. I tell you from that time until now, my dad has been cancer-free and without complications. I believe God honored my parents and me because we put Him first.

Matthew 10:32-39, "Whoever acknowledges me before men, I will also acknowledge him before my Father in heaven. But whoever disowns me before men, I will disown him before my Father in Heaven. Do not suppose that I have come to bring peace to the earth. I did not come to bring peace, but a sword. For I have come to turn a man against his father, a daughter against her mother, a daughter-in-law against her mother-in-law—a man's enemies will be the members of his own household. Anyone who loves his father or mother more than me is not worthy of me; anyone who loves his child more than me is not worthy of me, and anyone who does not take up his cross and follow me is not worthy of me. Whoever finds his life will lose it, and whoever loses his life for my sake will find it." I invite you to re-read these verses. I recognize they are difficult scriptures to read, but they tell us God requires us to lay down our lives for Jesus. Isn't that what He did for us?

God did not cause this situation, but He allowed it to happen at the beginning of the ministry, and even for the surgery to take place on the day I traveled. I saw this as a test of my devotion and commitment to Him. I believe if I had not recognized the devil was at work to delay and destroy what was important to God, and subsequently to me, and God was using this situation to prove my heart and my devotion, I could have missed what He wanted to do in my life and ministry during that season of time. I have witnessed this repeatedly throughout the many years of my service to God.

The next person God tested was Jeanette, one of our team members, who was already on the mission field when she was notified her sister was in a coma in the hospital and they feared she would not make it. We prayed with her, and she made the decision to stay and finish her assignment because she, like me, recognized God was fully aware of what was going on. When she arrived home, she went directly to the hospital and prayed for her sister. The next day I went to the hospital, and as I prayed for her sister the Lord told me to get right into her ears and to declare the words found in Psalm 118:17, "*I shall not die, but live, and declare the works of the Lord.*" A few weeks later, her sister walked out of the hospital totally healed, and is still healed today. This amazed the doctors and everyone who knew her condition. God honored Jeanette because she put Him first.

A few years ago, Daniel, one of my staff members, experienced a very similar situation. His younger brother, who had been sick for a while, took a turn for the worse, and shortly before we traveled to Haiti, he died. As one of my key people, Daniel was needed on the trip. He prayed while acknowledging that God is all-knowing, and if He allowed his brother's death a few days before he was scheduled to travel, then he had to make the tough decision concerning who was first in his life, God, or family. Without the help of his wife, he decided to keep his commitment to God and he told his family. Although many of them were not yet saved, they understood because they knew Daniel's devotion to God.

I tell you these stories because I want you to know you will face testing and tough decisions when God wants to do something amazing in your life. You will always be given the chance to decide who you will follow. Will you move forward with God or will you allow the distractions or ploys of the enemy to stop you?

Let's look at the story of Caleb. As we study his life, we will find a man whose belief in God was so secure that circumstances could not move him. He reminds me of the widow's story that I previously shared with you.

So the Lord said to Moses, send some men to explore the land of Canaan, which I am giving to the Israelites. From each ancestral tribe send one of its leaders. So at the Lord's command, Moses sent them out from the Desert of Paran. All of them were leaders of the Israelites. From the tribe of Judah, Caleb son of Jephunneh. They came back to Moses and Aaron and the whole Israelite community at Kadesh in the Desert of Paran. There they reported to them and to the whole assembly and showed them the fruit from off the land. They gave Moses this account: "We went into the land to which you sent us, and it does flow with milk and honey! Here is its fruit. But the people who live there are powerful, and the cities are fortified and very large. We even saw descendants of Anak there. The Amalekites live in the Negev; the Hittites, Jebusites and Amorites live in the hill country; and the Canaanites live near the sea and along the Jordan." Then Caleb silenced the people before Moses and said, "We should go up and take possession of the land, for we can certainly do it." But the men who had gone up with him

said, "We can't attack those people; they are stronger than
we are." And they spread among the Israelites a bad report
about the land they had explored. They said, "The land we
explored devours those living in it. All the people we saw
there are of great size. We saw the Nephilim there (the
descendants of Anak came from the Nephilim.) We seemed
like grasshoppers in our own eyes, and we look the same to
them."

Numbers 13:1-3; 6; 26-33 (NIV)

We are introduced to Caleb when Moses sent the twelve men to spy out the Promised Land. Caleb was not a natural-born Israelite; he was a Gentile who converted. He became a part of the tribe of Judah (1 Chronicles 4). In Numbers 32:12, and Joshua 14:16, Caleb's father is said to be a Kenizzite.

In Joshua 15:13 it says Caleb was given a portion/share among the children of Judah when they received their inheritance. His name means, 'Whole-hearted or faithful.' His name is a true reflection of his whole-hearted devotion and service to God. After the spies came back from spying out the land, Caleb and Joshua were the only two with the right report. Caleb was the first to speak up and say, "Let us go up and conquer the land." He believed they could, although there were giants in the land because he trusted God.

Caleb understood something the others did not—God was bigger than any giants they were facing. He did not doubt since God had given them the land, they would have the victory over every giant. He was a true leader who encouraged the people to follow God despite the opposition of the enemy. Although he was not a natural-born Israelite, his devotion and steadfast heart for the things of God, made him a *standout* among all the others, so God chose him. God will use anyone who will make themselves available to Him.

God handpicked him for this assignment and promotion because God knew what he would say as His people opposed Him. God used him because He was all about promoting God's goodness and power. In Numbers 14:24, God called Caleb, "My Servant." This title carried the highest honor given to anyone and had only been used previously to describe Abraham and Moses. God used this title to describe this man. In the eyes of God, Caleb was a true, righteous leader. He enthusiastically believed God and was passionate and devoted to Him. Caleb radically served God and tried to lead others into the same service. He conquered his enemies because he knew God was with him.

Zealous for God

What does it truly mean to follow God? Let's discover the keys through the life of Caleb.

> *Now then, just as the Lord promised, he has kept me alive for forty-five years since the time he said this to Moses, while Israel moved about in the desert. So here I am today, eighty-five years old! I am still as strong today as the day Moses sent*

me out; I'm just as vigorous to go out to battle now as I was then. Now give me this hill country that the Lord promised me that day. You yourself heard then that the Anakites were there and their cities were large and fortified, but, the Lord helping me, I will drive them out just as he said.

Joshua 14:10-12 (NIV)

Do you still get excited when you hear the mention of God's name? Do you still feel it is a privilege to serve Him in any way that He chooses? Have you felt at any time that, as a Christian, you are just simply going through the motions? I have experienced this feeling of just going through the motions at various times in my Christian journey. I found myself in this place because I was disappointed God had not answered my prayers when I thought He should have. I did what was necessary without the passion I had once exhibited. There were times I wondered why God was so distant. As a result, I found myself going through the motions of praying, worshiping, reading the Word, and going to church! I had lost my zeal and passion for the things of God, and just hearing His name did not cause my heart to respond with any great joy but only with tipped emotions.

I discovered this scripture during one of those dry seasons and it addressed my apathy. Revelation 3:14-16, *"To the angel of the church in Laodicea write: These are the words of the Amen, the faithful and true witness, the ruler of God's creation, I know your deeds, that you are neither cold nor hot. I wish you were either one or the other! So, because you are lukewarm—neither hot nor cold—I* *am about to spit you out of my mou*th." Can I tell you that this was a wake-up call for me? I was reminded of the tremendous sacrifice God made in sending Jesus to the cross and the HUGE price Jesus paid for me. I repented and began praying these words then, and still pray them today, "Lord, give me a love for worship, prayer, and your Word." He has been faithful in doing this, but I still must do my part and pursue Him daily.

Caleb did not burn hot and then cold toward God. He was steadfast in his zeal and commitment to Him. He was enthusiastic about who God was, and what He could do. He did not doubt God's power and His availability. When others gave a bad report, he refused to be part of that crowd. He was not afraid or intimidated about speaking up and going against popular opinions. Caleb did not keep quiet even when the majority of people did not agree with him. Some of us shy away from speaking up at times because we do not want to rock the boat and lose relationships. At other times we don't speak up because we want to keep the peace. Think about this with me. When you keep quiet even though you are being prompted by the Holy Spirit to speak, what is the end result for you? All of us must get to the place where we don't allow the enemy to silence our voices. Let's not miss opportunities to speak truth in whatever situations we find ourselves in. Remember, God will give you the right words to say.

Caleb was zealous for God. He did not lose his passion for what God assigned him to do. He made a complete break from the world and those around him to follow God. Often, we need to make a break from people and the world to truly hear and follow after Jesus. Caleb had also seen the giants in the

Promised Land but was moved only by his faith in God. He was unmoved by what he saw in the natural because he understood the supernatural power of God. Listen: twelve men were sent out but only two believed God could deliver on His promise. The others feared what they saw because their trust was not in God but in their abilities. Their abilities were limited compared to these giants. Caleb and Joshua remembered God delivered them from captivity and trusted He could do it again. The other ten forgot how great a deliverer God was and allowed fear to defeat them. These two men allowed God to lead them and did not depend on themselves, whereas the other ten led the people away from God. They did not obey His commands, and this resulted in an entire nation of people being delayed for years in the wilderness. Those ten spies along with that whole unbelieving generation did not enter the Promised Land.

You must examine your associations to ensure they will not lead you away from God. There are people in your life who may cause you to miss your destiny. Caleb and Joshua could see the blessings that were awaiting them in the Promised Land, but the others could not. All they saw were the potential problems, and this caused them to murmur and complain. These men wanted to stone the other two messengers who only shared the truth with the people.

~

Caleb Believed God

What made Caleb different from the others? Although he was also a slave, as were all the children of Israel in Egypt, when God freed him, he truly believed and received his freedom. He was free indeed and chose to embrace more than just his physical freedom. He walked out of the natural bondage in which he had existed and walked away from the spiritual bondages that had enslaved generations of Israelites. He was just as downtrodden as the others, but when he saw God's amazing miracles through Moses the scales fell from his eyes. He saw God clearly and acknowledged His greatness. Caleb knew without a doubt, with God on their side their victory was already assured! He reminds me of Isaiah, who in Isaiah 6 saw the Lord clearly for the first time after his earthly king died. There was nothing obscuring Caleb's or Isaiah's view of God. Caleb was a true believer who trusted in God's faithfulness. He did not doubt what God could do in their midst.

To wholeheartedly follow God, you and I must have a heart change. We must refocus on Him and reconnect our hearts to His. The other Israelites had physically left Egypt, but Egypt was still engraved in their souls. They yearned for the things of Egypt whenever they faced troubles or difficulties. They had not fully experienced a heart change and therefore could not embrace complete freedom. They chose to follow the leading of others but ignored the leadership of God. This generation was not fully convinced in their hearts that God could truly be trusted. Caleb however, experienced a true heart change that transformed him from the inside and out, and he yearned only after God.

~

A Man with a Different Spirit

> *The Lord replied, "I have forgiven them, as you asked. Nevertheless, as surely as I live and as surely as the glory of the Lord fills the whole earth, not one of the men who saw my glory and the miraculous signs I performed in Egypt and in the desert but who disobeyed me and tested me ten times —not one of them will ever see the land I promised on oath to their forefathers. No one who has treated me with contempt will ever see it. But because my servant Caleb has a different spirit and follows me wholeheartedly, I will bring him into the land he went to, and his descendants will inherit it.*

Numbers 14:20-24 (NIV)

I invite you to take another moment and reread the above passage. Here is my reason: God was hurt and offended by the treatment He received at the hands of the people He wanted to free. As you reread it, ask yourself, "Have I hurt God because of my disobedience?" If like me, you have hurt Him, just repent and make a turnaround towards obedience. God had to forgive the Israelites because of their unbelief. He said as surely as He lived and the Lord's glory filled the whole earth, not one of the men who saw His glory and miracles and disobeyed Him would enter the Promised Land. God said they treated Him with contempt. Contempt means disdain, dislike, disrespect, disapproval, scorn, hatred, derision, and condescension. Wow! God felt their contempt deeply and personally. Only Caleb received the full approval of God.

God called Caleb my servant and a man with a different spirit. I have only found the statement 'a man with a different spirit' spoken about Caleb in the Bible. In this verse, God spoke only about Caleb at first and only mentioned him going into the Promised Land. What I want you to see is this: Joshua was not mentioned until verse thirty and was mentioned following the second time God spoke about Caleb. God spoke glowing words about Caleb but only mentioned Joshua's name. I want to look at this for a moment. Joshua was the leader who was chosen to eventually take over from Moses, yet God focused attention on Caleb. He stood out in God's eyes because he boldly spoke up for Him. Is it possible Joshua was intimidated by the crowd, and fear kept him from speaking up first since he only spoke up after Caleb had spoken? Caleb was bold and courageous.

In Joshua chapter one, when Joshua began to lead God's people, God told him several times to be strong and courageous and not to be afraid. God spoke to what was in Joshua's heart— fear, not only of the giants in the Promised Land but also of the people he was leading. The words 'fear not' appear three hundred and sixty-five times in the Bible; one for each day of the year. I believe God is telling us, as He told Joshua, no matter what our difficulties, NOT TO FEAR. This is a word for today as our world is changing. Do not fear the plans and plots of the enemy and definitely don't fear the people you are leading. This holds true whether you are in leadership in the church or the world.

For almighty God to speak well of any of us would be a mark of His approval. He spoke well of Caleb and had it documented in the Bible for all to see. He is giving us a clear example of what to do as we serve Him. How did Caleb have a different spirit? He was like none other. He was a mismatch with the others around him and did not believe or act like them. He had a different nature—God's nature and had absolute faith in God. Caleb simply believed in Him and embraced the freedom God gave him. He did not long to go back to his old way of life but only wanted the new life God had for him. God's commandments were not burdensome or difficult for Caleb to follow. Caleb had truly experienced God and discovered there was none greater and nothing sweeter than trusting and obeying Him. Caleb knew God; he had hope in God. His heart was pure and open toward God, and His motivation was to always please Him.

With all that being said, Caleb had to wait forty years before he could enter the Promised Land because of the people with whom he was associated, the Israelites. He could not conquer the land by himself, so he had to wait until God removed the unbelieving generation and raised up a new generation of men who would trust and follow Him. He was ready but they were not, so he was delayed in receiving His blessings for forty years. Be careful about your associations because they can keep you from entering into your promised land, or delay you from receiving your blessings at the appointed time.

~

Caleb Claimed God's Promise

Now the men of Judah approached Joshua at Gilgal, and Caleb son of Jephunneh the Kenizzite said to him, "You know what the Lord said to Moses the man of God at Kadesh Barnea about you and me. I was forty years old when Moses the servant of the Lord sent me from Kadesh Barnea to explore the land. And I brought back a report according to my convictions, but my brothers who went up with me made the hearts of the people melt with fear. I however, followed the Lord my God wholeheartedly. So on that day Moses swore to me, 'The land on which your feet have walked will be your inheritance and that of your children forever, because you have followed the Lord my God wholeheartedly.' "Now then, just as the Lord promised, he has kept me alive for forty-five years since the time he said this to Moses, while Israel moved about in the desert. So here I am today, eighty-five years old! I am still as strong today as the day Moses sent me out; I'm just as vigorous to go out to battle now as I was then. Now give me this hill country that the Lord promised me that day."

Joshua 14:6-12 (NIV)

After Joshua and the army destroyed the thirty-two kings and the Israelites were given their inheritance, God had another assignment for them. God told Joshua there was still work to be done to drive out the rest of the Canaanites who had hidden themselves among the Israeli clans. God said He would drive out the rest of the enemies in the land He had given to the tribes of Israel. The Israelites only had to cooperate with Him, but they did not drive them out. Instead, they lived among them and became very corrupt. Caleb, however, cooperated with God and drove every enemy from the land of Hebron which was his inheritance. He refused to cohabitate with them and continued to follow God wholeheartedly in all things.

Caleb believed God. He overcame every difficulty, every hindrance, every naysayer, and every giant by his absolute faith in God. He expected God to keep His promises and God did not disappoint. It had been approximately five hundred years since God had promised the land to the Israelites, and He delivered on His promise. Although the older generation missed entering the Promised Land, Caleb in his old age not only entered but God kept him strong and healthy so he could enjoy his blessings. Caleb and Joshua were the only two from their generation who received the promised inheritance.

Caleb did not look back he only looked forward. He believed God when he was in the prime of his life and he still believed God when he was in his eighties. He stayed close to God, not deviating from His path. Unlike Caleb, some of our names will never be known publicly but the impact on our families, communities, nations, and other nations around the world can leave an indelible mark on the heart of God that will last throughout eternity. As we believe in Him, our lives will be forever changed.

There are modern-day men who believe God and won just as Caleb did. John Calvin believed God and was a pastor at only seventeen. George Whitfield believed God and was preaching to great crowds at twenty-one. Charles Hadden Spurgeon believed God and was a famous pulpit orator at sixteen and became a pastor at twenty-one. I encourage you to start believing God and He will begin to do greater things in your life.

I close this chapter with a story I read of a young man who was raised an atheist. He was training to be an Olympic diver and the only religious influence in his life came from his outspoken Christian friend. The young diver never really paid much attention to his friend's sermons, though he heard them often. His friend believed for his salvation and did not stop sharing the gospel with him even though he was indifferent to it.

One night the diver went to the indoor pool at the college he attended. The lights were off, but as the pool had big skylights and the moon was bright, there was plenty of light to practice by. The young man climbed up to the highest diving board and as he turned his back to the edge of the board and extended his arms out, he saw his shadow on the wall. The shadow of his body was in the shape of a cross. Instead of diving, he knelt and asked God to come into his heart. As the young man stood, a janitor walked in and turned on the lights. The pool had been drained for repairs and was empty. The moment he knelt, prayed, and declared his faith and belief in the Savior, his life was saved in many ways. How about you? Do you believe Jesus? Do you trust He has the best plan for you?

Remember, God never forgets His promises and He will fulfill His word in your life.

Just like Caleb, you can TRUST Him.

THE WAIT IS OVER

Do you feel like you have been in a waiting or holding pattern for a long time? Did you raise your hand? So did I. The waiting seasons of life can be unbearable for many of us. One reason is we don't know what is taking so long for our answers to manifest. So much of life is spent waiting. Waiting for God to move in our lives; waiting on answers to our problems; waiting on test results from the doctors; waiting for the manifestations of promises to come to fruition; waiting on difficult situations to change! We spend most of our lives waiting for things to happen to us. If we are not careful in the waiting seasons, we can lose hope and confidence in God's ability to help us. We can ask the questions—where is God? What is taking Him so long to show up in my difficult situation?

Since the fall of man, difficulties have become a consistent part of daily life. After Adam and Eve fell, they began to experience difficult challenges. Their once carefree life in God was now a battle to survive. Adam had to work hard tilling the ground to produce crops to sustain them. Eve began to experience pain in childbirth. Cain killed his brother, Abel, and they understood grief in its deepest form. They knew what it truly meant to endure loss and experienced the intense depth of sorrow. The death of one son and the expulsion of the other from their lives were heartbreaking. Jesus told us in John 16:33 that we would have tribulations but to be of good cheer, He has overcome the world. This means that during the painful struggles you are facing, Jesus has already won the victory for you. Because of the love He has for us, He has prepared us for what is to come. Trouble would be part of our daily lives; life was not always going to be smooth sailing; there would be difficult bumps in the journey, but with all these challenges we can cheer up because just like Him, we will overcome.

Isaiah 40:31 tells us God gives strength to the weary and increases the power of the weak. We will get weary at times, but we must refuse to give up. When life hands you hard things to deal with, they are designed not only to delay you but to destroy you. Yet, you still have a choice to make—will it make you better or will you be destroyed? As you wait you must decide, will I be bitter and angry or will I simply trust God has me securely in the palms of His hands, and no circumstance can pluck me out of them. It's your decision, your choice.

The only way to deal with difficulties is to face them head-on. Jesus faced death. He looked at the horrible things He would suffer and still chose to die in our place. Some blame

God when they encounter difficulties. They reason since He is God and is all-powerful, He should keep them from harm. They forget we live in a sinful, fallen world, and the devil has come to steal, kill, and destroy us (John 10:10). In the same verse, Jesus said He has come so we can have life and life more abundantly —life overflowing. What you must know is this—even though God allows the difficulties, He does not cause the difficulties. He will be with you through these unbearable times. We must, with the help of the Holy Spirit, take our eyes off the problems and refocus our hearts on God who is the solution to every problem we face.

We often hear this statement, 'God works in mysterious ways, His wonders to perform'. Although this is not a verse in the Bible, Romans 11:33 puts it this way, "*O the depth of the riches of the wisdom and knowledge of God, how unsearchable are his judgments, and his ways past finding out.*" You will find throughout the Bible God is always working whether we can trace His movements or not. He is never inactive but is working things together for those who love Him. Because He is not idle, you can expect some 'suddenlies' in your life. Suddenly after years of waiting, your promise manifests. Suddenly after giving up hope, He comes in and restores your hope. Suddenly after a long season of waiting you are set free. Suddenly He performs a miracle in your life that amazes everyone including the doctors. Suddenly He causes you to get the promotion when you thought it would never happen. Suddenly a loved one gets saved and turns their life around, bringing peace to both their and your soul. Suddenly your financial blessings come and you are rescued from painful struggles. You get the picture, He is working.

We know God can do all we ask Him to do. The challenge we have is we do not understand His perfect timing for our lives. 2 Peter 3:8 says, *"One day is like a thousand years to the Lord, and a thousand years are like one day."* Along with putting our trust and hope in God, we must trust His perfect timing for our lives even when the wait seems unending. You can be assured of this—whatever He has promised you, you will receive. There are many stories in the Bible that will help us to wait with expectancy. In this chapter, I want to look at one of them. Often when we think of John the Baptist's birth, we focus on Zechariah as the main character and not necessarily on his wife, Elizabeth. However, I want to draw your attention to her part of the story and focus on the long waiting season in which she found herself. Journey with me through her life and you will discover the faithfulness of God even when He allows us to wait.

> *In the time of Herod king of Judea there was a priest named Zechariah, who belonged to the priestly division of Abijah; his wife Elizabeth was also a descendant of Aaron. Both of them were upright in the sight of God, observing all the Lord's commandments and regulations blamelessly. But they had no children, because Elizabeth was barren and they were both well along in age.*
>
> *Luke 1:5-7 (NIV)*

The story of Elizabeth reminds us God is listening. If there was someone in the Bible who needed to anchor their hope in God, it was her. Her name means satisfaction or abundance, but there was no manifestation of this in her life for years. She was the daughter of Aaron, Moses' brother, the high priest. She was a descendant of the priesthood, and her rich heritage meant she had direct access to God, yet she struggled. She was married to a priest, but she still had to pray and wait for God's perfect timing in her life. We can concede struggles are great equalizers in people's lives and no one is exempt. They affect the just and the unjust, the rich and the poor alike. Struggle is color blind. Like birth and death, we will all experience it in one form or another. Although we will face struggles, they can be overcome if we have our lives anchored in Jesus Christ.

This statement bears repeating. Elizabeth was the High Priest's daughter. She was married to a priest but could not produce an heir. The stigma, shame, and embarrassment must have been unbearable. In her century, barrenness was considered to be a curse from God. Keeping in mind in that century they usually married young, around thirteen to fifteen years old, the scripture says Zechariah and Elizabeth were old. Historians estimate they were probably in their sixties.

So, let's do a little speculation. If they were in their sixties and were married in their teenage years, then we are looking at over forty-plus years of barrenness. We can only imagine the struggles and hopelessness that must have been a part of their daily lives, especially Elizabeth's. People considered her to be cursed even though she had such a rich lineage. Her struggle reminds me of Hannah's struggle to conceive Samuel. As I shared in Chapter 4, Hannah's harassment by an enemy in her household, her husband's second wife, plunged her into a season of hopelessness and depression.

Our difficulties are made worse because our enemies do not leave us alone in the struggles. They often harass and torment us to the point where we experience depression. God, however, will give you victory over your enemies and use your struggles to produce greatness in your life.

Elizabeth did not know God had a great plan for her barrenness and the delays she was experiencing. Delays are not denials, just holding patterns while God is working on the details of your life. She did not know she would give birth to a son in old age, who would be renowned as the forerunner of Jesus Christ. Like many of us, she was living in hope and believing God would hear her desperate prayers for help. If the historians' estimate of their age is correct, then compared to others in the Bible they had one of the longest waiting seasons I have found.

Jesus waited thirty years to begin a three-year destiny. Abraham waited twenty-five years to produce an heir. Before ascending to the throne, David was on the run for approximately thirteen or fifteen years. John the Baptist, the forerunner of Jesus waited approximately thirty years to begin his ministry of preparing the way for the Messiah. Are you seeing the pattern? Waiting is a part of life. It is a part of the journey to our destinies. Waiting is necessary to develop us—our character, devotion, trust, and faithfulness to God prior to Him promoting us. Elizabeth had given up hope in the waiting, but

God was not finished with her yet. His delay had a great purpose attached to it.

The Angel Said

While Elizabeth was home tending to her duties, God decided it was time to birth His purpose, John the Baptist, into the earth.

Once when Zechariah's division was on duty and he was serving as priest before God, he was chosen by lot, according to the custom of the priesthood, to go into the temple of the Lord and burn incense. And when the time for the burning of the incense was come, all the assembled worshipers were praying outside. Then an angel of the Lord appeared to him, standing at the right side of the altar of incense. When Zechariah saw him, he was startled and was gripped with fear. But the angel said to him: "Do not be afraid, Zechariah; your prayer has been heard. Your wife Elizabeth will bear you a son, and you are to give him the name John. He will be a joy and delight to you, and many will rejoice because of his birth, for he will be great in the sight of the Lord. He is never to take wine or other fermented drink, and he will be filled with the Holy Spirit even from birth. Many of the people of Israel will he bring back to the Lord their God. And he will go on before the Lord, in the spirit and power of Elijah, to turn the hearts of the people to their chil-

dren and the disobedient to the wisdom of the righteous—to
make ready a people prepared for the Lord."

Luke 1:8-17 (NIV)

God sent Gabriel to visit Zechariah while he served as a priest before Him. God knows all you do in service to Him, and He will dispense blessings into your life in the midst of your service. At times, some people simply pray and wait for God to move but may not be proactive while waiting.

For several years, my ministries were home-based. I prayed daily for God to provide an office space for us to expand the work, but He delayed, in my opinion, for a long season of time. One day as I was praying in frustration, I informed Him I had been waiting for a long time for Him to move without any results. Very quietly and firmly the Holy Spirit said to me, "You are not waiting on me, I am waiting on you to move." All the times I prayed; I thought God was not ready to move but He was waiting on me to take a step of faith. As I moved, He backed my efforts and gave the necessary provisions. I had delayed myself because I thought He would give me the money needed beforehand to pay the bills. I failed to realize I was required to walk by faith and not by sight. It was not until I took a step of faith that the provisions began to come in.

In the first three years of stepping out in faith, getting an office space, and hiring a few staff members to help me with the work, God demonstrated His faithfulness. Although the journey was difficult and stressful at times, God paid every bill for the ministries, including staff and myself. My faith began to grow. Psalm 27:33 says, *"The steps of a good man are ordered by the Lord."* This is what I discovered in those years of waiting. It is not in the longing we have for God to do something, the hoping He will move, in our constant waiting, or even in our continual praying that God moves; it is the *steps* you take that He directs. To get God's attention, and for Him to open the doors for which you are praying, you must take a step of faith.

Zechariah and Elizabeth received their blessings while he was doing something—serving. He was doing what God had assigned him to do even though he had not yet received the thing for which he prayed. The angel Gabriel, who visited Zechariah, said his *prayer* was heard. Not prayers, *prayer*. Do you think it is possible they only prayed once during their forty-plus years of waiting? No. I believe God answered the first prayer they prayed. He simply answered it years later.

Isaiah 60:22 says, *"I am the Lord; in its time I will do this swiftly."* Everything has a time frame. We simply do not know what God's timeframe is for manifesting His answers in our lives. We have to wait. We have to keep praying. We have to keep trusting. We have to keep hoping with expectation until we see the manifestations. God did not tell Elizabeth on this day He was going to visit her husband and give them the blessing of a son. She had no warning the day had come according to God's timetable to bring forth a major miracle in their lives and in the earth. God simply did what He does often —moved suddenly in their situation.

After Gabriel spoke to him, Zechariah did what some of us would have done after waiting so long; he did not believe and spoke out his doubt. It is one thing to be doubtful in our minds, but when that doubt is spoken out of our mouths, we can empower the enemy to delay or even stop what God wants to accomplish through us. Zechariah's lack of faith caused him to lose his voice for nine months. Gabriel suspended his speech because, I believe, this kept him from aborting his blessings with doubt-filled, negative words.

Think about something you sincerely wanted to happen in your life. The longer it was delayed, you may also have doubted and then wondered out loud if it would ever come to pass. We all, at times, forget we are created in the image of God. We neglect to realize we have His nature, and we have the ability to speak things into existence. In Genesis 1, God spoke words and the world, and all living things came into existence. You have His nature, and according to Mark 11:23, He has given you power to speak to the situations in your life and they must obey you. We must keep guard over our words. Stopping Zechariah's speech was a dramatic move by Gabriel, but it is a great lesson for all of us not to voice our doubt or unbelief. Doubt nullifies our hope and expectations, and even cancels the manifestations of God's blessings in our lives.

Imagine with me how shocked Elizabeth must have been to find her husband mute. Give me a little creative license here: let's suppose she heard the door open and called for Zechariah but received no response. She probably went looking for him to see why he had not responded, only to discover he could not speak. She knew immediately something dramatic had happened to him. He probably had to tell her this wonderful news with hand gestures or in writing. If she had any doubt, she would become pregnant in her old age, she kept her mouth firmly shut and did not speak her doubt or she could have been rendered mute like her husband. John had to be born, and God would not allow them to stop His plans from unfolding in the earth.

There are plans God has for your life, but you must check the words you are speaking over your future. Do you feel unqualified for what God is speaking to you about your future? Do you have thoughts you may not be well received when you step out in faith? Are you concerned with not getting all the words you are speaking perfectly enunciated? This is how God dealt with me when I exhibited fear and concerns about walking through the doors He was opening for me.

Here are some questions I asked Him. What if my words don't come out right? What if I stumble? What if my messages are unclear and people don't fully comprehend them? What if I am not well received? Do you have as many 'what ifs' as I did? Let me turn this around. What if God fills your mouth with the right words that change lives? What if He speaks through you with great power and authority? What if your testimony impacts many hearts and changes destinies? What if someone on the verge of desperation hears your story and is rescued from destruction? These are just some examples of what He has done for me.

Don't let the lies the enemy is whispering in your ears stop you from being used by God. God corrected my thinking. He challenged me about who I was attempting to glorify, me or Him. He said, "Is this about you looking perfect, or about me working through your imperfections to bring glory to My name?" Fear and doubt can cripple us if we give way to them.

Elizabeth chose to embrace the words Gabriel spoke to Zechariah and she conceived.

I want you to see what Elizabeth did after conceiving. Luke 1:23-24 says, "When the time of service was completed, he returned home. After this his wife Elizabeth became pregnant and for five months remained in seclusion." She did not go and broadcast her pregnancy news to her relatives, friends, or neighbors. Even though Elizabeth knew people thought she was cursed by God because of her barrenness, she did not tell them this great news. She had the most wonderful testimony to share—God had a greater, more perfect plan for her life, but chose to keep it to herself. She could have gotten vindication and satisfaction after sharing this, yet she remained quiet. I am painting a picture for you.

What I see is she took time to savor this wonderful thing God had done. Elizabeth recognized her God had done the impossible for her and taken away her disgrace from among the people. She discovered God's favor had been with her all along, even when she could not see or feel it. She had to wait to experience this great miracle, so she kept it secret for a while. It is also possible she may have been concerned after all this time, and in her old age, something could possibly go wrong with the baby. She was human after all, and just like many of us may have faced some uncertainties. Whatever her reasons for keeping the news to herself, God demonstrated His faithfulness to her after tremendous hardships, and a long season of waiting, hoping, and praying.

The Visit

John's destiny was intimately linked to the destiny of Jesus. This is the reason Elizabeth had to wait. She had to wait until God was ready to birth Jesus into the earth. She first had to wait for Mary to be born and then wait until she was old enough to conceive, approximately thirteen years old. Had John been born any sooner or any later, He would have missed his assignment of being the forerunner of Jesus. God's timing for our lives is perfect, even though it is hard to believe while we are waiting.

After Mary conceived, the angel told her about Elizabeth's pregnancy. Elizabeth was a relative, yet Mary did not know of her pregnancy until this precise moment. Why share this news with her? To encourage her faith! To show her if God would do this great thing for Elizabeth, then God would manifest His promise in her life also. Remember, Mary was not yet married. She would face many hardships in her journey; therefore, God comforted her.

Mary hurried to visit Elizabeth. Upon her arrival, and at the sound of her voice, the baby John leaped for joy in Elizabeth's womb. Capture this. Upon hearing Mary's voice John, who was only in the womb for six months, responded because he recognized the Messiah was in his presence in the womb of Mary His mother. Consider the scripture says Mary hurried to see Elizabeth. We can conclude Jesus had only been in the womb for a very short time, yet His presence caused a great reaction. Elizabeth was instantly filled with the Holy Spirit and began to prophesy that Mary was the mother of her Messiah, Jesus.

In Luke 1:14-16 it also says this about John, *"And thou shalt have joy and gladness; and many shall rejoice at his birth. For he shall be great in the sight of the Lord, and shall drink neither wine nor strong drink; and he shall be filled with the Holy Ghost, even from his mother's womb and many of the children of Israel will he turn to the Lord their God."* Did you see it? John was filled with the Holy Spirit while in the womb of his mother. God begins the work in our lives before we are conceived (Jeremiah 1:5). He continues to work on our futures and destinies even while we are in the womb. It is also evident to me we need the Holy Spirit to successfully fulfill our destinies.

I wonder if, before the arrival of Mary, who was carrying the Messiah, John had ever moved in Elizabeth's womb before. If not, then this was a confirmation not only to Elizabeth but also to Mary that God was with them, and their sons would usher in a new season of great joy and also great sorrows in their lives. The moment John leaped; Elizabeth discovered John was alive and well. I wonder if she understood what a force He would be in the earth for God. She knew, however, that God was with him.

Luke 1:56 says Mary stayed with Elizabeth for about three months and then returned home. It is possible Mary may have been there to witness the birth of John. Remember, Elizabeth was six months pregnant when she arrived. After witnessing this miracle, and seeing the faithfulness of God, Mary went home encouraged and ready to face the many difficulties that awaited her as an unwed woman. She understood, however, that God would see her through. She must have recognized no one would be able to take her life prematurely since Jesus had to be born.

As John was already born and ready to fulfill his destiny, so also Jesus would be born to fulfill His destiny in the earth. Can you see how truly awesome God is? How He cares deeply about us? He set the stage to build Mary's confidence and give her the necessary grit she would need as she faced a perilous journey, and He will do the same for you.

After Elizabeth gave birth, her neighbors and relatives heard the Lord had shown her great mercy, and they shared in her joy. Elizabeth made it through years of waiting, difficulties, defeat, hopelessness, and embarrassment. Her amazing God who appeared to have abandoned her for many years showed up and used her powerfully, giving her beauty for the ashes that used to be her life. He lifted her out of the pit of shame and disgrace, and He gave her a testimony, and just like Hannah and Mary, a son who has been renowned for generations. Centuries later we are still hearing the name, John the Baptist. Out of the endless waiting came great purpose. All those who laughed, mocked, scorned, and judged Elizabeth because of her barrenness, their children passed from history without a mention, but John the Baptist lives on even today.

What are you waiting for God to do in your life? I know the waiting season can be intolerable and unbearable at times. It feels like you are never going to get your breakthroughs as you face one difficulty after another; but never forget, that God is with you, and He will come into the midst of your difficult circumstances and bring you out. As you continue to anchor your hope in Him, He will not forget your labor of love or your prayers. I encourage you to keep holding on, your answer and your help are on the way because Jesus promised to hear and answer you when you pray.

Remember, in the midst of frustration, depression, and hopelessness, God will give you the victory and a testimony that will make people marvel about your God.
Your testimony will bring many to the saving power of Jesus Christ.

Just like Elizabeth, you can TRUST Him.

JESUS RESCUED ME

Has anyone ever rescued you from a difficult or painful situation? They were a lifesaver for you when you felt as if there was no hope. I can think of many seasons in my life when I needed help from God and others. These seasons of helplessness and even hopelessness can cause you to feel as if no one can or will help you. When help does arrive, you must acknowledge you were never truly alone; God was with you throughout the painful journey. I am reminded of a number of times when I was either sick or had surgery. During those times when the pain was excruciating, someone helped to meet my needs. They were unable to reduce my pain level, but they were there, and their assistance helped ease the emotional pain.

Recently, while I was ministering in another city, I had some problems with my right arm. It became frozen and the pain was almost unbearable. I went to an all-night clinic and the medicine they gave me did not help but simply upset my stomach. Before accepting this assignment to minister, I was told a lady at the church where I was scheduled to speak was going through some severe health challenges and they were extremely concerned for her. She had requested a meeting with me and although I was in severe pain and my stomach was upset and unsettled, I felt I could not leave the city without seeing her and addressing her needs. One of my staff members and I met with her, and she shared her struggles.

I counseled her and then walked her through some inner healing prayers that were filled with scriptures concerning what God said about her healing. She is still young and not ready to die; she feels there is much more she can do for God. At the conclusion of our time with her we anointed her, laid hands on her as we are told in Mark 16:18, and prayed the scriptures over her for her healing. As I closed the prayer, I was reminding God of Isaiah 55:11 which says, *"So is my word that goes out of my mouth: it will not return to me empty but will accomplish what I desire and achieve the purpose for which I sent it."*

I then declared Psalm 118:17 that she would live and not die and declare the work of the Lord. While I ministered to her, my pain level was off the chart but God sustained me. The moment I finished I became very sick. That day, God demonstrated His power in this lady's life, and He used me even though I also needed rescuing from pain. We left knowing God would be faithful to rescue her. I am happy to report it is a year later and she is still alive, her health is improving; God is demonstrating His love and compassion to her each and every day.

From what do you need rescuing? I can assure you even though you may be going through painful times, Jesus is with you. I have also discovered over many years of serving Him at times the journey will require a few sacrifices. Some people may reason since they are serving Him, they should not have to go through the same challenges unbelievers endure—sicknesses, financial struggles, emotional hardships, etc., yet we experience them. Matthew 5:45 says it rains on the just as well as on the unjust. This means believers and unbelievers alike will experience good times and difficult seasons in their journeys. The difference between believers and unbelievers, however, is we have help as we face these unbearable times. This lady had help. She had her family, church family, and above all, God was always with her.

Think about the sacrifice of Jesus on Calvary. He was sinless yet He suffered. He did not have to go through the horror He endured but He chose it so we would be free. Hebrews 9:22 says without the shedding of blood there is no remission for sin. His sacrifice was necessary for our freedom. Following Jesus requires sacrifices. Like Jesus, you and I will have to lay down our lives, take up our crosses, and follow Him daily (Matthew 16:24-26). We will have to say *no* to many things; no to the enemies' strategic plans of deception and destruction; no to our fleshly desires; and no to the temptations that are staged to pull us away from an intimate relationship with Jesus. You will need to say *no* as often as is necessary until the devil knows you mean business and will stand your ground against him.

It is the enemy's job to try and stop you from having an intimate relationship with Jesus, but it is your job to remind him who you are in Christ and to stand against him. All of us will be tried, tempted, and tested by the devil, and will have to resist him using the Word of God. If we do not stand up to him, we will live in defeat. How do we fight against his tactics? We use the Word of God against Him just as Jesus did in the wilderness. Psalm 119:11 says, *"I have hidden your word in my heart that I might not sin against you."* Make sure the Word is deeply embedded in your heart because only with the Word will you counteract the attacks of the enemy.

As you seek to be used by God, the personal attacks will be great at times but you are equipped for victory. Each of us must make a decision about following Jesus wholeheartedly. The woman with the alabaster box of perfume poured her all on Jesus. Journey with me as we study her life, and at the same time ask yourself, "What will I pour out on the Savior?"

Help Is Available

> *Now a man named Lazarus was sick. He was from Bethany, the village of Mary and her sister Martha. This Mary, whose brother Lazarus now lay sick, was the same one who poured perfume on the Lord and wiped his feet with her hair.*

> *John 11:1-3 (NIV)*

John identifies Mary, Lazarus' sister, as the woman who anointed Jesus with perfume. Jesus set her free from demonic possession

—He cast seven demons out of her. When Jesus encountered her in her lowest condition, He did not condemn her but forgave and released her from the bondage of sin and slavery to the devil. The number seven indicates the totality and completeness of the demonic possession she was under. How she became so totally possessed by the devil is unclear, but she was under his absolute control and struggled to make decisions that would lead her out of darkness and into a place of peace and fulfillment.

Mary understood her life of sin was against the law, that she was guilty, and the penalty for being caught in sexual immorality was death, yet she could not seem to control herself. Jesus told her to leave her life of sin but she had no power within herself to do this. Her freedom from demonic possession could only come from Him. When she came to anoint Jesus, she was filled with gratitude, love, and appreciation for all he had done to free her.

> Luke 7:47 tells us it was only after she washed His feet that He forgave her sins. Imagine with me the guilt she must have felt; the burden and shame she carried; how weighed down she must have been with all the sins of her past. As she wept, those tears were a reflection of the burden of guilt and shame she had carried throughout her life.

She felt worthless. In forgiving her, Jesus restored her worth and dignity and gave her a new life. He made her whole— complete, unbroken, restored, with nothing missing from her life anymore.

Jesus did more than rescue her. He set her on a path that would forever lead her to fulfillment. As she accepted her freedom, she would begin to live a life that glorified Him and would point others to Him. At first, Mary may not have recognized the magnitude of the gift of freedom she received, since she had lived in bondage for such a long time.

Imagine with me how she must have felt after He forgave her. It is how you feel each time you are forgiven—unburdened, weightless, able to breathe because there is no longer a millstone around your neck. She could raise her head and look others in their eyes for the first time in a long while because there was no longer anything in her life that needed to be hidden. She was free—free to be herself. If she was anything like the woman at the well who Jesus freed in John 4, she became a testimony of what a changed life looks like. People were able to see from her transformation she had encountered something or someone greater than herself. This is who Jesus is and this is what He does. When we encounter Him, we too will be forever changed.

I say this conclusively: if you have met the risen Savior and you are unchanged then ask yourself this, did I really meet Jesus? There is no way you can encounter Jesus and not be changed forever. Think about those in the Bible who met Him and who they became afterward—Peter, James, John, blind Bartimaeus, Paul, and the widow at Nain, to mention a few. The widow at Nain was on the way to bury her son when in great compassion Jesus stopped the funeral procession and raised her son from the dead. The list of people whose lives

Jesus changed while He walked the earth is too numerous to list.

I encourage you to study Matthew, Mark, Luke, and John, and document the many changed lives that are written on these pages. He is still changing lives today. I want you to know this—He will change you and your loved ones as well. No one is beyond His reach, no matter what they might have done. There is absolutely no sin He will not rescue us from. There are no depths too deep that He will not enter to ransom and redeem us, so find your hope in this today. Mary was in the depths of sin and Jesus reached in and rescued her.

The Alabaster Box

Now one of the Pharisees invited Jesus to come and have dinner with him, so he went to the Pharisee's house and reclined at the table. When a woman who had lived a sinful life in that town learned that Jesus was eating at the Pharisee's house, she brought an alabaster jar of perfume, and as she stood behind him at his feet weeping, she began to wet his feet with her tears. Then she wiped them with her hair, kissed them and poured perfume on them.

Luke 7:36-38 (NIV)

When Jesus accepted this invitation to dinner, He was fully aware God had set the stage for Him to affect and impact the lives of these Pharisees. Have you discovered yet that God does not waste a single thing that happens in your life? He will use all of it—struggles, failures, and victories for His glory and to advance His kingdom if we just allow Him to use us.

Jesus was willing and ready for God to use all His experiences to advance the kingdom's message. Remember, the Pharisees did not care for Jesus' doctrine or all the miracles and signs He performed. Therefore, it is interesting He would be invited to dinner with them and to accept. What I see happening here is Jesus was willing to go into places where He was not fully accepted in an effort to add people to the kingdom of God.

There are times when God will move us out of our comfort zones and make us uncomfortable if this will advance His message and impact lives. I remember telling God I was happy to minister the gospel message but not to send me to the mission field. I even reasoned with Him, saying, "I don't like the heat or bugs." But who won out, me or God? Can I tell you He knows us way better than we know ourselves? One of my greatest joys is to take the gospel message around the world, and to love, feed, and clothe the lost and the hopeless—God's precious children. I am so glad God did not listen to me but uses me as He wills.

Let's look at how this woman accepted discomfort. Without knowing it, she had walked into an assignment for the advancement of God's kingdom that would impact generations to come. She gave her all even though she was in an uncomfortable spot.

Alabaster was made from stones that were commonly found in Palestine. It resembled white marble and was one of the precious stones used in the decoration of Solomon's temple. Perfumes, oils, and ointments were often put into alabaster vessels because it kept them pure and unspotted. Alabaster was very expensive.

As Mary broke it to pour the contents on Jesus, the Pharisees as well as the disciples began to murmur and complain, calling what she had done wasteful. Historically, alabaster was a symbol of purity and great honor. Is it any wonder Mary would pour this on Jesus? In today's market, the price of the perfume would be worth a year's wages. Think about this. Would you give Jesus a year's wages—all you had worked hard for? Many of us would reason we could not afford to do this. How would we survive? How would we pay our bills? How would we eat? Mary did not hesitate to give Him what was valuable to her.

In going to the Pharisee's home Mary broke with normal tradition. How did she hear about the invitation? Some Bible passages say Mary was the sister of Lazarus, whom Jesus had raised from the dead. Possibly this was how she knew. When she learned of the invitation, she put a plan into motion. She decided to crash the party. It was unheard of for women to attend one of these events. Their role was to prepare the food for the guests. I am sure Mary did not share with anyone else what her plan was.

It was customary in those days when you invited guests to dinner; a slave would wash their feet free of the dust from the journey. Each guest would be greeted with a kiss, and their head would be anointed with oil. As Mary observed the arrival of Jesus, she noticed no one kissed Him; no one washed His feet, and no one anointed Him. God set a perfect stage for her to act. He gave her the right opportunity to serve the One who had set her free. Let's unpack the boldness she had, and what it took to walk into that room, effectively breaking every custom and tradition in order to serve Jesus.

In that century it was not the norm for a woman to approach a man. A woman could not invite a man out or over to her home for dinner. She could not kiss a man in public, and definitely could not approach a man especially one with such a high-ranking role in society. This was a private dinner and no one had invited her, not only because she was a woman but because she had a stained reputation. God, however, invited her to this dinner and then set the stage to glorify His Son. It is evident Mary had not planned what she would do when she arrived and was presented with the opportunity. It is also evident she had no idea how she was going to anoint Jesus. She did not bring anything with which to wash or dry His feet, which tells us this was not her original plan. Something broke in her heart as she anointed Him and pushed her into a deeper place of worship. She seemed unprepared but that was not the case. Having a basin, water, and towel would not have had the deep impact of what she actually did.

Mary did not approach Jesus from the front but from behind. She felt unworthy to face Him directly, and since no one had done what was customary and washed Jesus' feet, she did. Since no one had welcomed Him with a kiss, she kissed His feet. Since no one had anointed Him, she poured the perfume she had earned on Him. Consider this perfume was possibly what she may have used as part of her trade. She not only gave her heart away to Jesus but also her means of making a living.

As she kissed His feet, the tears began to flow. Tears of regret; tears for the loss of her dignity; tears for the many lost years of her life; tears for being held in bondage for so long; and tears over the many regrettable decisions she had made with her life. She not only poured her perfume on Jesus, but she also poured her pain, heartbreak, hurts, and her deep regrets on Him. As she performed this humble task, she also poured tears of thanksgiving, love, and gratitude on Him for delivering her from the seven demons that had so completely possessed her. Her tears were her thanks to Him for saving her from sin, and the ultimate punishment of being stoned to death. How overwhelmed she must have been.

Since she had no towel to dry His feet, she used her greatest commodity, her hair. 1 Corinthians 11:15 tells us that a woman's hair is her glory. In Jesus' century, although women generally had long hair, it was almost always tied up in some way with bands, braided, or in knots. This was because women in pagan cults would let their hair down in frenzied worship of their gods. Mary's hair was probably bound until she set it free and used it to dry Jesus' feet. She used her most precious gift on the Savior. She probably had only planned to pour the perfume on His head to anoint Him, and then leave, but God captivated her heart and led her into a deeper worship of Him. Even if she had only planned to go in and hurriedly perform this duty; as she worshipped Him the worship became so intense, as is often the case when we remember from how much He has redeemed us. She lingered in her worship of the King.

May this also be our experience as we worship the Savior—we take our time in worship of Him. She did not allow the onlookers whose stares were penetrating, accusatory, and even disgusting, to cause her to rush in an effort to avoid them. Listen: when you are in the presence of the Savior, everything else melts away. Do not hurry through your worship, prayer, or time spent in His Word. This time of deep connection will provide more healing in your life than anything else that may be tugging at you.

Like Mary, allow your worship to be deep, personal, intense, and impactful, and let it be something that is meaningful to God and life-changing for you. All who saw her were either pierced in their hearts or angry at her boldness. God was watching and was pleased with her worship and devotion. Remember, people are observing you even while you are unaware you are being watched. Her act was one of selflessness, faith, gratitude, true worship, and deep devotion.

We can well imagine what was taking place in the hearts of the men who were gathered for the dinner. Most of them probably knew of her and her damaged reputation. There would be consequences later if they got a hold of her. Not only did this time of service cost her financially, but it would also cost her personally.

In addition to her humility, there were other costs to pay. She would be rejected, scorned, and gossiped about. She would be accused by these self-righteous leaders of crashing this man's gathering but this did not deter her. If looks could kill, I am sure Mary would not have survived this encounter with these religious men. Galatians 2:20 describes Mary. It says, "*I am crucified with Christ and I no longer live, but Christ lives in me. The life I live in the body, I live by faith in the Son of God, who loved me and gave himself for me."* She had laid down her life in that moment for Jesus. She gave her life away for Him. She knew these religious men would not want to be in the presence of a sinner such as her, but that did not deter her from boldly forging ahead.

Her desire to worship, anoint, bless, and give thanks to Jesus was greater than being looked down on or being rejected. Her worship meant everything to her. When she finished her task, there was nothing left of Mary; she had left it all at the feet of Jesus. Although she had emptied herself at His feet, she left His presence full to overflowing with love and forgiveness. She was completely free.

Jesus Defends Mary

Jesus' defense of Mary was a teaching moment for the disciples and the guests who were gathered for the dinner. Jesus taught them and us about judging those who are attempting to make a life change.

When the Pharisee who had invited him saw this, he said to himself, "If this man were a prophet, he would know who is touching him and what kind of woman she is—that she is a sinner." Jesus answered him, "Simon, I have something to tell you." "Tell me teacher," he said. "Two men owed money to a certain moneylender. One owed him five hundred denarii, and the other fifty. Neither of them had the money to pay him back, so he canceled the debts. Now which of them will love him more?" Simon replied, "I suppose the one who had the bigger debt canceled." "You have judge correctly, Jesus said." Then he turned toward the woman and said to Simon, "Do you see this woman? I came into your house. You did not give me any water for my feet, but she wet my feet with her tears and wiped them with her hair. You did not give me a kiss, but this woman, from the time I entered, has not stopped kissing my feet. You did not put oil on my head, but she has poured perfume on my feet. Therefore, I tell you, her many sins have been forgiven—for she loved much. But he who has been forgiven little loves little."

Luke 7:39-47 (NIV)

Simon's critical thoughts about Mary were known to Jesus, so Jesus addressed them. Jesus did not shy away from this controversy because there were others in the room who were thinking the same critical and judgmental thoughts about what she had done and who she was. Simon was not only judging Mary but he was also questioning Jesus. If Jesus was truly a prophet, He would know who and what manner of woman this was who touched Him.

Simon was thinking Jesus did not have any discernment and insight, until the precise moment when Jesus read his mind and spoke the answers to his unrighteous thoughts. Simon was more critical of Jesus than the woman. He judged the authenticity of Jesus. He assumed Jesus did not know the woman was a sinner, and made the wrong assumption that if He did, He would have nothing to do with her. Since Jesus accepted her, he thought Jesus must not be a prophet after all.

Remember, the Pharisees were very critical and judgmental of others. They were very pious and standoffish. They thought they were better than the average person. Simon concluded since Jesus was not a prophet, they did not have to listen to Him or receive His teachings. When Jesus read his mind and knew his thoughts, this proved to him and all the others that Jesus was who He said He was—the Son of God, their Messiah. I am sure Simon was startled Jesus knew his intimate thoughts so completely.

What Simon and the others did not yet understand is Jesus loves all people. He came to seek and save those who are lost. Even as the Son of God, Jesus did not think of Himself as better than those He came to serve. He humbled Himself to win mankind to God. He got involved in people's struggles. He went into the pit of sin and rescued them. He healed those who did not ask Him for healing just because He had compassion for them. He set those who were demonically oppressed free because He did not want the devil to continue terrorizing them. Jesus raised people from the dead because He wanted to heal wounded hearts and souls. He rescued Mary because she was wounded and lost but God had a purpose and destiny for her. God never planned for His daughter, Mary, to be so overcome by the evil one or to live so far below her privilege as His daughter. She was His creation and a rare treasure on the earth.

She had not discovered how special she was until Jesus stepped into her life and freed her.

Jesus pointed to the things Simon had not done when He entered his home. Then He pointed to the fact that Mary had humbled herself and given Him more than Simon had. She outdid Simon in every way with her humility and service. Jesus gave us one of the most powerful scriptures in the Bible when He said because she had been forgiven much, she loved much. When we realize how much we have been forgiven, we will love much, give much, and do away with habitual sin in our lives as did Mary.

Some lessons in this story will enhance our lives and take us into a deeper love relationship with Jesus. The love and grace of Jesus are not logical, and we cannot reason it away. People will shun us because of our sin but Jesus loves us despite all we have done. Jesus loves even the greatest of sinners. Mary was not competing with the others in the room as she served, but she outdistanced them all with her humility and her absolute devotion to our Savior. Our pursuit of Jesus strengthens and deepens our worship of Him. True, life-changing worship always happens at the feet of Jesus because we make ourselves lower than Him in that position. Mary went to the feet of Jesus, and this is the place we must all go to begin honoring Him for all He has done for us.

When you understand what grace has accomplished for you, then genuine worship will flood out of your heart toward the Savior. Worship involves your heart, soul, mind, and emotions. We give Him all we have because He has given all He has to us. Mary came to Jesus with a repentant heart, and He did not turn her away. It was after this intense worship that Jesus told her that her sins were forgiven. He had previously delivered her, but after she laid herself bare at His feet, He gave her what she needed the most to move forward into a fully changed life—forgiveness.

Jesus loves sinners, and because He does, He willingly laid down His life for every one of us. Luke does not tell us that Mary spoke during her meaningful worship. Words are not necessary when our hearts are overflowing with love and gratitude for all Jesus has done in our lives. Mary's tears, her shame, her unworthiness, and even her fear of being rejected could not keep her away from Jesus. What she did spoke volumes to those in the room and to generations that followed.

True worship of God can never be hindered or stopped by your critics or any negativity, because it is from the heart.

Mary Magdalene pursued Jesus with all her heart, and she won her freedom. We see in Luke 8:1-3 she journeyed with Jesus and supported His ministry. In both Mark 15:40 and John 19:25 we learn she was at His crucifixion. In John 20:1 she was at the resurrection and was probably numbered with the one hundred and twenty who were in the upper room waiting on the coming of the Holy Spirit. She never turned back once she became free and was steadfast in her devotion from the day Jesus delivered her. May her story of being transformed from the inside out inspire and challenge us to give our all to Jesus. May we never look back but only move forward with boldness and tenacity as we make Jesus known to our families, friends, co-workers, and strangers—people whom God will bring across our paths. May we anchor our hope and trust securely in Him, knowing He will never leave us broken and lost.

Remember, Jesus loves all people, even the greatest sinner. He has come to seek and save those who are lost.

Just like Mary Magdalene, you can TRUST Him.

WHO TOUCHED ME?

~

Some people in our world have not experienced the loving touch of another person, and this may include you. They don't know how it feels to be encouraged or supported. Some children have not felt a loving touch or even had a hug from their parents. What you will find is people who are deprived of this most basic human support will, at times, find it difficult to connect with others.

Years ago, I knew a lady who up until the age of twenty-five had never received a hug or heard the words I love you from anyone in her family, including her parents. Her parents provided for her needs while she was growing up but she was never affirmed either by words or with hugs.

She shared that the first time she received a hug was when she went to a church, and a greeter welcomed her with a hug as she entered the building. Since this was the first hug she could recall, her initial response was to recoil since she did not understand why a stranger would so freely embrace her. Can you relate to this story? This lady was generally friendly and engaging but she had also built a wall around herself. This touch from another believer caused her to realize there were things missing in her life. After attending this church for a while, she began to open herself to the hugs that were being lavished on her and to reciprocate them. As the years went by, she grew in her understanding of the basic human need to be touched.

She discovered it is God's desire for each of His children to experience not only the depth of His love but love and affection from others. God also wants us to remove the barriers that surround our hearts and allow Him deeper access into our lives.

Jesus touched and healed many people throughout the Bible. He understood the value of connecting with people not only on a physical level but emotionally and spiritually as well. Why is a touch so important to us? It is a well-known scientific fact hugging induces oxytocin, which is the hormone known for reducing stress, lowering cortisol levels, and increasing a sense of trust and security. According to a recent research study conducted at the University of North Carolina, women who received more hugs from their partners had lower heart rates and blood pressure, and higher levels of oxytocin.

Scientists are discovering what God has known for eons of time—people need to be touched. Just think with me about the birth of a baby, and what I will call the continual hug they received while in their mother's womb. These babies feel secure, cared for, and loved while in the womb. One of my co-workers recently became a grandmother and she shared how the doctor quickly laid the baby on her daughter-in-law's bosom right after the birth, so the bonding could begin to take place immediately.

I propose to you it was not so the bonding could take place, but so the bonding would continue uninterrupted. As human beings, we need human touch to encourage us, and to help us to connect at a deeper level with people, which then leads to greater trust. Being touched helps to promote better health and to ward off diseases. It also helps us to bond with others whether they are family members or part of a team. Being touched more often will keep some people from living in depression, and help others feel more encouraged and supported. My friend, who experienced her first hug at church, continued at that church for years and grew in her interactions with others.

In my book, *Lord, Make Me Whole*; I shared a brief synopsis of the story of the woman with the issue of blood that was recorded in Mark 5. I want to explore her story in greater depth in this chapter. She touched Jesus and as a result, she was made whole. As you touch Jesus whether through praise, prayer, worship, or the Word, you will also be made whole in all areas of your life.

Warfare in Our Souls

Have you ever received a bad report of any kind—about an unexpected death, a sickness, divorce, or the loss of a job? Devastating, right? When the report comes it often causes paralyzing fear, worry, and anxiety to rise in our hearts. The attacks on our bodies and emotions affect our souls, and if we are not careful, they can affect our spirits as well. It is the enemy's plan to bring destruction to your life.

John 10:10 says, "The thief comes only to steal, kill, and destroy, but Jesus said I have come that you may have life, and life until it overflows." When you receive a report from the doctor, what they give you are the facts, but you have something greater than facts, you have the truth. Truth is what Jesus has already said about you and the situation. Truth is—knowing and being fully convinced He has conquered sickness, and by His stripes you are healed. Truth is—He will give you victory and will see you through every difficult trial. Truth is—He will never leave you nor forsake you.

Scientists have discovered there are thirty-nine root causes for diseases on the earth. Jesus bore thirty-nine stripes on His back which provide for our healing—one for every root cause. This tells me for every report of sickness you receive from the doctors; the true report is by the stripes of Jesus you are healed. We have to overcome fear to embrace the promise that we are healed. Someone defined fear as false evidence appearing real. It looks and feels real but it is not. You will have to do battle with the enemy for what God has given you—your health, marriage, family, finances, and even your purpose on the earth. Remember, a defeated enemy has no power to defeat you unless you give him that power.

Your mind is the control center of your life. You have the ability to harness the thoughts in your mind first before they become a reality. You determine if you will allow negative, harmful thoughts to control you. Whatever you allow to take hold of your mind will take hold of your life, and it will ultimately control you.

2 Corinthians 10:5 says, *"To cast down vain imaginations and every high thing that exalts itself against the knowledge of God and to bring every thought captive to the obedience of Christ."* You win or lose the battles first and foremost in your mind. If you are unable to gain victory over your thoughts, you will speak them out, and then act on the ones that are rampaging through your mind. Before anyone ever commits a heinous act, the thought first originated in their mind, and they did not control or master it. As a result, they acted on it and the effects were often disastrous. This holds true for either the positive or negative.

In the same way, God can drop a word or a thought into your mind and as you meditate on it, you will begin to believe it, then speak it, and ultimately it will become a reality in your life. I often tell people when they come to one of our events that they are sitting in or participating in a thought God planted in my mind years ago—the ministries. I believed what He spoke to me concerning the ministries and then moved out in faith to implement them. As I meditated and prayed over the ministries for a long period of time, I ultimately spoke about them to others, and they became a reality.

Your thoughts are powerful and will change your life either for good or for bad. I want to explore the life of the woman with the issue of blood, because she gained the victory in her thoughts first, and then received the manifestation of healing in her body.

> When Jesus had again crossed over by boat to the other side of the lake, a large crowd gathered around him while he was by the lake. Then one of the synagogue rulers, named Jairus, came there. Seeing Jesus, he fell at his feet and pleaded earnestly with him, "My little daughter is dying. Please come and put your hands on her so that she will be healed and live." So Jesus went with him. A large crowd followed and pressed around him. And a woman was there who had been subject to bleeding for twelve years. She had suffered a great deal under the care of many doctors and had spent all she had, yet instead of getting better she grew worse. When she heard about Jesus, she came up behind him in the crowd and touched his cloak, because she thought, "If I just touch his clothes, I will be healed." Immediately her bleeding stopped and she felt in her body that she was freed from her suffering.

> *Mark 5:21-29*

How do you gain victory? You must act on what Jesus tells you. In this passage of scripture, Jesus was on his way to Jairus' house to heal his daughter when this woman interrupted Jairus' miracle to get her own miracle. Jairus' daughter was at the point of death, yet Jesus stopped to heal this woman. Jesus will allow you to interrupt Him so He can perform a great miracle in your life.

The woman had spent everything she had looking for a cure but was still sick, and now she was broken. She heard the stories of Jesus' healings, and God dropped a divine revelation into her heart. If she could just touch the hem of Jesus' robe, she would be made whole. This was a 'Rhema' word, a specific word spoken from the mouth of God directly into her heart. In Greek, the word Rhema means an utterance or a thing said. She heard the word that was spoken to her and applied her faith towards touching Jesus. When she went to Jesus, she was not looking for an audience with Him. She was not trying to tell him all she had suffered; she just wanted to touch His robe. She knew if she touched even His clothes, based on the revelation she received, she would be healed.

Let's think about what it took for her to get to this moment in her life. Years of struggling without any cure! She was beset by fear, doubt, worry, and anxiety. I am sure the moment she received the revelation, the enemy began his attacks in her mind as he always does with us. How could she possibly think she could get to Jesus? She was too sick and too weak. Besides, there was always a huge crowd around Jesus, especially men. She knew if she was caught out in the crowd, and the people discovered she had a blood disease, she would be stoned to death. Having a blood disease during that century meant you were unclean (it was a religious issue) and had to stay away from others. Her life was at stake either way—without healing, she could die due to loss of blood, so she figured she had nothing to lose. She probably could not tell anyone her plans because of the danger of it getting out, so she had to undertake this by herself. She probably had no prayer support as she undertook this journey, so could not ask for help to get to Jesus in her weakened condition.

These difficulties would have caused many of us to give up without trying, but not this woman. She was desperate for a miracle and her desperation drove her to do something that was out of the ordinary and plain illegal.

When she found Jesus, He was of course surrounded by a crowd of people. Think with me—how was she going to get to Jesus? She was not tall or big enough to push her way through the crowd plus she was weakened by the loss of blood. The enemy was probably harassing her concerning what could happen if she was discovered. Have you ever wondered why God told her to touch the hem of Jesus' robe instead of any other parts of His clothes? Do you not think wherever she touched Jesus, she would have received her healing because of the power that was inherent in Him? I have pondered on this numerous times. Why did God make this so difficult for her? Consider with me there was no viable way to reach the hem of Jesus' robe while standing up; therefore, she would have to get on her knees. In her weakened condition, she began her search looking for the hem of Jesus' robe. Many people wore robes in that century as it was the dress code. The crowd was tight, so she had to do some work to get her miracle. As I read her story, I am reminded of the children that both Elijah and Elisha raised from the dead. These mothers had to do something to produce their miracles.

One woman had to feed Elijah her last meal while trusting God to provide (1 King 17:7-24). The other woman provided a room in her home for Elisha to stay. When her son died, she had to journey by donkey for thirty miles, from Shunem to Carmel to get to Elisha, so he could come and raise her son from the dead (2 Kings 4:8-37). They each sowed into their own miracles. Let me say it again. They had to do something to get the results they sought. This applies to us also. Sometimes God will do the entire work Himself but at other times we must participate to get our results.

The woman with the issue of blood was sowing time and effort to receive her miracle. I am sure the enemy was telling her, as he does with us, that she was wasting her time. Nothing would come of this venture. Jesus does not care if you are struggling. You will not receive what you have been praying for all these years. If Jesus was going to heal you, He would have done it already. Do any of these things sound familiar? We have all experienced his harassment when we faced difficult times. You have to keep God's Word paramount in your life during these times. Declare His promises over and over again until they take deep root in your soul. She kept pursuing the revelation she knew God had given her, and as a result, she gained the victory.

Jesus felt power leave His body, and He asked, "Who touched Me?" The disciples were amazed He would ask such a question seeing the crowd was so large. People all around were touching Him. There was something, however, they did not know about this touch—it released power out of Him. Jesus knew this was no ordinary touch. This was an unusual touch. It was not a touch of curiosity. This was not someone who just wanted to touch Him because He was Jesus. No, this was a touch of desperation. This touch was from someone who needed healing. This person understood He was their only hope, the only answer, and the only one who could heal. Jesus was her last and only hope.

Her desperate need pulled power out of Jesus. She had believed God's prompting and applied her faith. She applied her faith when she left her home to find Jesus; she applied her faith to get through the crowd; she applied her faith when she began searching for His robe, and her faith was rewarded. She came trembling to Jesus and the entire crowd heard her testimony.

Some people were probably appalled she would dare to come out in the crowd with a blood disease, but this did not stop her from telling her story. Jesus said, "Daughter, your faith has made you whole, go in peace." He called her daughter. Can you hear God, the Father, addressing His precious daughter through the words of His Son? He had been with her through all those years of struggles. Not once had He been unaware of where she was as she faced one trial after another. At no time had He taken His eyes from her. He had known exactly where she was and sent Jesus at the right time, to the right place, and with the right words to heal her. He wanted her to know He had not ignored her prayers. Listen: couldn't God have simply healed her all those years ago? Sure, but then you and I would not have this powerful example that our Savior will also heal us.

Jesus told her that her faith had made her whole. What does it mean to be made whole? She was complete, with nothing broken in her life or body any longer. Being whole means her finances were also restored. She was undiminished because of her struggles and could go back to enjoying life because her blood issue was cured. The things that were missing in her life were once again realigned in her body. He had done a complete restoration not only of her health but also of her emotions. Consider the emotional toll she had been under for years, and to have that burden lifted was a gift beyond compare. She had interrupted Jesus to receive her miracle and she won. She won over the struggles in her body, mind, thoughts, and emotions.

Some of us may think Jesus is too busy to stop and give us a miracle. You must overcome this doubt. Know He is willing and ready to be interrupted at any moment to give you your miracle. He will stop, address your condition, and come to your rescue. He will even delay an urgent situation, if necessary, to address your needs. This woman triumphed over the lies of the enemy and her story has been told for centuries. She had enough faith to overcome all the odds against her. Why did Jesus not tell us her name? Because she could be anyone of us with an issue only He can handle.

Are you facing a situation no one but Jesus can handle? I invite you to spend time in His presence, and then ask the Holy Spirit to remind you God is a healer. He has a Rhema Word for you that will change your health, your wealth, your situation, and your life. Based on

Hebrews 4:12, the Rhema Word is a living, active word that

is sharper than any two-edged sword. I told you earlier it is defined in Greek as an utterance or a thing said. It is a spoken word. You must declare it over your situations. This is a specific word God gives to you in the midst of a crisis or a difficulty, so you can combat the attacks of the enemy.

Here is an example: when sickness comes upon you, out of hundreds of scriptures in the Bible, God may give you just one or two to stand on and to confess over yourself. When you embrace the Scripture and begin to speak it out loud, it will bring healing to your body. It is your sword against the attacks of the devil.

Remember, Jesus is available for you, so stop and ask Him for His help. He will respond to you.

Just like the woman with the issue of blood, you can TRUST Him.

NEVER GIVE UP

~

Have you ever faced what seemed like an impossible task? As you looked at what you needed to accomplish, you felt like giving up even before you started. There are seasons in life when we face things that wear us down. These things are designed to stop us from persevering to our victorious end. At times, we have exerted all our strength and are worn out by the effort to accomplish these tasks. In the midst of the struggles, we can get discouraged and may want to quit. Sometimes we feel there is no point in continuing, and if we do decide to continue, we may choose only to put forth the minimum effort. At other times, we may pray for God's help to overcome these obstacles, so we can get better results. During these times you will find God is available to help you. You will also discover what may be impossible for you is definitely possible with Him.

When God gives you an assignment, He fully understands you will need Him in order to successfully accomplish it. He wants to be intricately involved with you in its fulfillment. Ask yourself, "Am I fulfilling my part or attempting to do His part?" Remember, there are things only God can do, and the things He assigns to you, you are capable of handling with His help. Hebrews 10:35-38 says, *"So do not throw away your confidence; it will be richly rewarded. You need to persevere so that when you have done the will of God, you will receive what he has promised."*

As you are persevering, you must hold on to your confidence in God. Your journey is not in vain, there is a reward at the end for a job well done. You will receive His promises for your life. Why does God require us to persevere? Because it is developing attitudes in our lives—character, faithfulness, strength, and tenacity. These will help us reach a victorious end and cause us to receive all the promises that are assigned to our lives.

Perseverance helps us get stronger: stronger in our thoughts, emotions, character, and physical makeup. Through perseverance, we grow and become better than we were. When God gives us an assignment, He equips us to complete it. If He allows a situation that is causing you to have to press harder towards its accomplishment, then He knows this will produce good fruit in your life. The enemy cannot bring anything into your life that God does not know about. If God allows it to come to you, He knows the fruit this will birth in and through you to impact others for Him.

Galatians 6:9 says, *"Let us not become weary in doing good, for at the proper time we will reap a harvest if we do not give up."*

The scripture acknowledges we are prone to get weary as we persevere. It encourages us to not allow weariness to set in and overtake us. It's important to note it says we can get weary even while doing good, meaning things that benefit others; things that advance the kingdom of God; and things that are helping those struggling in life. As I type these statements, I think of the many people who are caretakers to elderly parents and struggle under the immense workload. I also think about those who have had to deal with family members who are enduring severe sicknesses. In these shocking situations, Jesus tells us not to get weary while doing these good things. How is it possible to keep weariness at bay? By seeking His help at all times, by allowing Him to work alongside and in you; by casting your cares on Him moment by moment because the Bible tells us He cares about us. He wants to yoke up with you, so He can help you to carry your heavy load (Matthew 11:30).

I am reminded of an elderly lady I met in a grocery store a few years ago. I had left my grocery basket for a moment and when I returned to it, she was holding on to it and would not let go. She thought this was her basket and we were shopping together. When I realized she suffered from Alzheimer's, I tried to locate the people to whom she belonged. I couldn't help wondering to myself how they had allowed her to wander off without supervision. She began to follow me throughout the store as I attempted to find a store employee to make an announcement for her family. Then she started touching people and a few of them reacted with irritation before I had a chance to explain she was having some health struggles.

Finally, an elderly man came looking for her. He was extremely irritated she had wandered off and he yelled at her, grabbed her hand, and pulled her away. This was a man who was struggling with weariness while doing good. A few minutes later as I went into another aisle, there she was again by herself playing with a teenager's hair. The mother of the teenager simply did not know what to do. I stopped and explained her struggles, and someone would come and get her. The elderly gentleman showed up again, still overcome with irritation. Let's walk in his shoes for a moment. He was having to take care of her (possibly his wife), while she was oblivious to what was going on around her. He was persevering through difficult times and his weariness was evident.

Jesus wants to help you with weariness. He says if you do not give up, then at the right time you will receive a harvest. Our challenge is we do not know when the right time is, so we have to persevere until we get to it and receive the reward. This requires help that only Jesus can give us. Listen: God only ever asks us to do our part. He never asks us to do what He alone can do. As you do your part, persevering, He will give you the breakthroughs. Perseverance is not easy but it is necessary.

~

Perseverance Is A Must

Have you ever had to persevere through hard, difficult times? I believe perseverance is the key that unlocks the doors in our lives and gives us entrance into God's blessings. If you give up when the way is paved with difficulties, you will miss the greatest opportunities to know God and His Son in a rich and fulfilling way. Perseverance means to abide, be steady, endure, to be patient, to persist, and to not give up.

> 1 Corinthians 15:58 says, *"Therefore, my dear brothers, stand firm. Let nothing move you. Always give yourselves fully to the work of the Lord, because you know that your labor is not in vain in Him."* The scripture tells you to be steady, let nothing move you, stay on course because you are not laboring for anything.

In a race, the person who persists and never gives up in the face of adversity will always triumph. I saw this clearly while ministering in Guatemala. If you have never been to Guatemala, one of the things you should know is it is very mountainous. As we traveled from city to city, I prayed intensely as the van struggled up these mountains that were so steep, that I feared we would tip over. During one of these trips, I saw a lady carrying a stack of wood on her back up this extremely steep mountain. She was almost bent over at the waist as she climbed. You could see the struggle and the hardship on her face. In that moment I cried out to God for her and others like her who are facing such tremendous hardships.

This woman was persevering because she had no other options. There were no other recourses before her. She had to do what was necessary to keep surviving. I said to the Lord, "I know it was never your plan for humanity to struggle so hard to survive life, please help your children." In that moment, I felt the intense love and compassion of the Father for His children. His love was deep and powerful, and I asked, "What do you want me to pray?" Have you ever spent any time asking God what is on His heart and what He wants you to pray for? I encourage you to ask Him. You will find He has a prayer agenda —things you can pray about daily. Things that are crucial for the lives of His children, not only those in your home but in communities around the world.

Perseverance is not a 'one-time' thing, it is constant. You have to keep at it until you overcome it. People who persevere will succeed because they refuse to give up even when the odds are against them.

Our Christian life is a race. We are not jogging aimlessly but have a purpose for being in the race—eternity with Jesus. We are not in a full-out run to the finish line; we are sprinting to it day by day as we race to gain the prize. Therefore, it will take perseverance and endurance to finish your course well. Do not allow life's difficulties or trials to disqualify you from finishing your race well. Your goal is to cross the finish line into the bosom of the Savior.

1 Corinthians 9:24-27 says, *"Do you not know that in a race all the runners run, but only one gets the prize? Run in such a way as to get the prize. Everyone who competes in the games goes into strict training. They do it to get a crown that will not last, but we do it to get a crown that will last forever. Therefore I do not run like a man running aimlessly; I do not fight like a man beating the air. No, I beat my body and make it my slave so that after I have preached to others, I myself will not be disqualified for the prize."*

Did you notice in the scripture you are the only one who can run your race successfully? And did you also see you are the only one who can disqualify yourself from finishing the race? No matter the obstacles you are facing, the one thing you must be sure of is this—you have already WON. You have won because Jesus won it all for you. He went to the cross and He conquered death, hell, and the grave. Be confident of this: He who began a good work in you will carry it on to completion until the day of Christ Jesus. He will finish what He started in you and will not leave you incomplete. He will not leave you struggling where He finds you but will accomplish His work through you. The suffering, struggles, and hardships you are persevering through will produce good results in your life. Run the race; stay on the course; finish well. Don't disqualify yourself. You will then receive a glorious welcome at the end of your race.

~

Not Abandoned

While we are in the struggle, we may feel as if God has abandoned us but He has not. Most of us do not understand why He allows us to go through the struggles, so we must hold on to Him in the midst of them. There are, however, those who will let go of Him in their difficult trials. If we are honest, some of us have felt He has left us to fend for ourselves when the pain was unbearable. John the Baptist's parents gave up hope for a child because there was a long delay before the manifestation came. Let's dig into their story together.

> *In the time of Herod king of Judea there was a priest named*
> *Zechariah, who belonged to the priestly division of Abijah;*
> *his wife Elizabeth was also a descendant of Aaron. Both of*
> *them were upright in the sight of God, observing all the*
> *Lord's commandments and regulations blamelessly. But they*
> *had no children, because Elizabeth was barren; and they*
> *were both well along in years.*
>
> *Luke 1:5-7 (NIV)*

In chapter 7, I shared the struggles of Zechariah and Elizabeth to birth a son, John. In this chapter, I want to look at who John was and the exemplary life he led. He fulfilled his kingdom assignments even though he faced many difficulties. There were great struggles as he walked out his purpose but he did not give up. There are only a few instances where God gave specific names to children in the Bible, and John the Baptist was one of them. John's name means Jehovah has been gracious and has shown favor. Remember I said God named him. Therefore, although Zechariah and Elizabeth waited over forty years for his birth, God in naming him John declared He had been gracious and shown favor to them.

You will hear me say this many times, "We understand a number of things about God, but we do not understand His perfect timing for our lives." God essentially declared He had done what He promised, even though they had to wait an extraordinarily long time. At no time prior to the arrival of Gabriel to speak to Zechariah did God tell them His plan for them. Unlike Abraham and Sarah, who knew a son was forthcoming; Zechariah and Elizabeth had no idea that God in His infinite wisdom had already made the decision to give them a son, so they had given up. They were like us, always praying and trusting God for a breakthrough.

As the forerunner of Jesus, John's birth was perfectly timed by God. He entered the world at the precise moment God had established for him. He was the voice crying in the wilderness, calling the people to repentance as he waited for Jesus' appearance. Historians say John began preaching at the age of thirty. This was the same age Jesus began His public ministry. You can see God's perfect alignment of these two lives for His purpose. John had one message—repent! He was radical in preaching it: not hesitant, fearful, timid, or intimidated by the religious folks. He was bold and courageous as he did what God chose him to do—to call men back to God through repentance. Many during John's century expected Elijah to return and proclaim Christ, so they were not welcoming of John.

In Matthew 17:11-13 Jesus told us who John was. In Matthew 17:10 the disciples asked Jesus why the scribes said Elijah must come first, *Jesus responded Elijah had already come, and just as they did not recognize Jesus, they did not recognize him. The disciples realized Jesus was telling them John was Elijah. John came in the spirit of Elijah.*

Malachi chapters 3 and 4 give us several prophesies about John's appearance. The Lord said He would send His messenger who would prepare the way before Him. He talks about coming near to the people for judgment because of their sins and waywardness. He said He would send the prophet Elijah before the great and dreadful day of the Lord's coming. Seven centuries earlier, the prophet Isaiah also prophesied about John saying, the voice of one crying in the wilderness: "Prepare ye the way of the LORD; Make straight in the desert a highway for our God."

As with Jesus, there is not much known about John before the age of thirty. God prepared him for his kingdom assignment in total seclusion. This should speak to our hearts—God does His work in our lives in secret as He prepares to launch us into our kingdom assignments. Matthew 11:18 tells us John did not come eating or drinking, he was not a social butterfly, nor was he trying to make friends or be popular. John was not trying to impress anyone or become a part of the in-crowd. He was single-mindedly calling men to repentance. John was intentional in his assignment. He dressed weirdly, so he stood out and apart from the others. He did not look like the other pious, religious people, nor was he trying to upstage Jesus when He appeared. John ate weird foods. He did not contaminate himself with worldly things; he was a walking sermon.

Let me ask a question. How does such an unsociable person draw the crowds he drew and baptize the many people he did? He was ordained by God to do exactly what he did, and because of his obedience, God caused him to be fruitful in his assignment. There are no records of John performing any miracles, as did Jesus and the other apostles, yet he was powerfully used by God. He baptized thousands who were drawn to him because of the one message he preached—repentance. His ministry reminds me of the passage in John 12:32 where Jesus says, *"If I be lifted up from the earth, I will draw all men to me."* John pointed men to Jesus. He lifted Jesus high and as a result, the Father drew the people to hear the message that would set them free.

Although Zechariah and Elizabeth might have felt abandoned by God as they waited for a son, God was perfecting the things that concerned them. He did not abandon them but gave them a son who was one of the greatest men to ever walk the earth. He has been renowned throughout history because of his, and their steadfast devotion to God. As a result of all their waiting, they left us a tremendous legacy of faith, faithfulness, devotion, and steadfastness to God. A legacy that John the Baptist carried on throughout his life.

John was Radical

From the moment John the Baptist stepped into the Jordan River, he was a powerful demonstration of what being radical is all about. He caused others to believe in the soon coming King because he was convinced of who Jesus was; the Savior of the world. Since there is no mention of John receiving a direct word from God about his destiny, it is apparent his parents prepared him to live out his purpose of being the forerunner of Jesus. His one radical message—repent. He challenged the Jews to turn from sin. He wanted them to be regretful for the way they were living. John called them to have contrite hearts before God.

John declared the kingdom of God was at hand. Isaiah had previously prophesied in Isaiah 40:3 that he was the voice crying in the wilderness, preparing the way of the Lord. His message was not a feel-good, encouraging message, it was one that brought immediate conviction to the hearts of men. His message was a wake-up call to many who had abandoned their service and devotion to God. John made no apologies for the hardness of the words he preached. The people needed to hear a strong word to shock them back into an awareness of how far they had strayed from God, and how disrespectful they had been to Him and His laws. God was offended at their vile practices of worshipping idols, sacrificing lame and sick animals to Him, and not loving and serving Him wholeheartedly after all He had provided for them (Malachi 1:6-11). Therefore, John did not hesitate to rebuke them and did not concern himself with offending them.

When he saw many of the Pharisees and Sadducees coming to his baptisms, he called them a generation of vipers—a venomous snake, a spiteful and treacherous people. Why this harsh description? The Pharisees were known as the separated ones and had the most influence among the people. They wore robes to distinguish and make them easily recognizable. They were haughty and arrogant, and despised those they did not consider their equal.

These Pharisees believed they were the only interpreters of God's Word and believed in predestination with a final reward for good works. This is the reason they bitterly opposed and fought against Jesus. They hated Jesus' message of equality and believed He was trying to make them common like the other people around them. WOW! That is really thinking too highly of themselves as we are told not to do in Romans 12:3. Jesus strongly condemned their hypocrisy, their salvation by works, and their lack of love for the common man—their neighbors. Remember, love is the essence of who Jesus is, so these people did not come close to representing the love of the Father for all mankind. Gamaliel, Paul's teacher, was a Pharisee, as were Paul and Nicodemus, yet they turned their lives over to the Lord Jesus Christ.

The next group of self-righteous people John dealt with were the Sadducees. They were all about following the law and rejected many traditions. They did not believe in life after death, the spirit world, or the immortality of the soul. The Sadducees had the highest level of the priesthood during that century. John was very familiar with their ways and called them vipers. He told them to bring fruit that showed a desire for repentance. John essentially said their fruit was not an outward expression of a transformed heart or deep inner conviction. He felt they were coming to be baptized without a true heart change. He told them without fruit—there is no real repentance.

Matthew 7:20 says, *"By their fruit, we will know them."* They needed to have their hearts pricked and changed, and John did not see this change in them. He told them of the coming judgment and warned them of the results of living unrighteously. He did not mince his words but was straightforward and direct. John understood the ultimate consequence of their sins if repentance did not take place. He was snatching them out of the kingdom of hell and was willing to do and say whatever was necessary to shock them into an awareness of how far they had drifted from God's laws. He wanted to see transformation take place in their lives. Unlike many people in our culture today, John was not trying to be politically correct. He saw people headed toward destruction, and since he had the solution for their salvation, Jesus, there was no hesitation in telling them how to change their ways.

Let me issue a challenge to you. Think about your family members, other loved ones, and friends. Are you allowing the light of Jesus Christ to shine through you to impact their lives? Are you speaking to them about their lifestyle? Are you warning them about the days of tribulation that are to come; and are you sharing with them the reason Jesus came and died in our place? If you are not feeling as emboldened as John to snatch them out of the hands of the enemy, ask God to give you that boldness. He wants them saved.

During a Bible study, a friend shared this testimony about how one of her daughters and her husband were once sold out to Jesus, and serving in ministry, but have since backslidden and were no longer following Him. They are very resistant to her sharing anything about Jesus, therefore she simply prays for them. When she goes to family functions, they make this statement, "Here comes Jesus' sister." This description of her is priceless and it brought great laughter from the crowd. Without her saying a word, her mere presence brings conviction to her children. I want you to know sometimes you will not need to speak a word for people to recognize they are not living as they should. Your presence is a living epistle (Bible) (2 Corinthians 3:2) they can read and know they are headed in the wrong direction. Are you Jesus' sister or brother? Can your loved ones see Him reflected in you? May we be ready both in and out of season to share His love, grace, mercy, and compassion not only to those we love but to all those around us. We must simply live Jesus before them and let Him do the work of convicting and changing their hearts.

John the Baptist's example is of a person who had only one purpose for living—to lead people to the saving knowledge of Jesus Christ. He was radical in his devotion and service, yet something happened that caused him to question if Jesus was the Messiah. Keep reading to find out about his faith struggle.

~

John's Struggles

So Herodias nursed a grudge against John and wanted to kill him. But she was not able to, because Herod feared John and protected him, knowing him to be a righteous and holy man. When Herod heard John, he was greatly puzzled; yet he liked to listen to him. Finally the opportune time came. On his birthday Herod gave a banquet for his high officials and military commanders and the leading men of Galilee. When the daughter of Herodias came in and danced, she pleased Herod and his dinner guests. The king said to the girl, "Ask me for anything you want, and I'll give it to you." And he promised her with an oath, "Whatever you ask I will give you, up to half my kingdom." She went out and said to her mother, "What shall I ask for?" "The head of John the Baptist," she answered. At once the girl hurried into the king with the request: "I want you to give me right now the head of John the Baptist on a platter." The king was greatly distressed, but because of his oaths and his dinner guests, he did not want to refuse her. So he immediately sent an executioner with orders to bring John's head. The man went, beheaded John in the prison, and brought back his head on a platter. He presented it to the girl, and she gave it to her mother. On hearing of this, John's disciples came and took his body and laid it in a tomb.

Mark 6:19-29 (NIV)

Throughout his life and ministry, John pointed to Jesus and prophesied about Him. His message was a cutting-edge message. We do not read much about John actually prophesying, but he did. He prophesied the kingdom of heaven was at hand. The Greek word for at hand is 'engus' and means 'near'. John did not want people to think they had many years ahead of them to accept Jesus. He knew tomorrow was not promised to anyone (James 4:14-15), so he clearly told them the coming of Jesus was near, so they could change their wicked ways. In Matthew 3:7, he prophesied about the coming wrath and told them about the ax that was laid to the root of the tree. He was speaking of the destruction of the nation and was saying God would cut down any trees that did not bear fruit and throw them into the fire. He spoke of unquenchable fire. He told them of the eternal pain they would suffer in hell.

John spoke about a fan in the hand of the Lord. This fan was the winnowing shovel with which the harvested grain was tossed into the wind to separate the kernel from the chaff. He was warning them there was coming a greater separation of the righteous and the wicked and the appearance of Jesus would bring this division. You can see he was a prophet in his own right.

John clearly knew who Jesus was. He was completely sold out to the belief Jesus is the Messiah. He was radical in his belief and spoke strongly about sin. Because He was bold and tenacious in his teachings about righteousness and holiness, it cost him His life.

The reigning King Herod Antipas was the son of Herod the Great, who had slaughtered infants in an attempt to kill the baby Jesus. This king listened to John's messages. He feared John and considered him to be a holy man. When Herod went to Rome he visited his half-brother, Phillip, and lusted after Phillip's wife, Herodias. He influenced her to leave her husband, and he divorced his wife leading to an unlawful union John boldly and unapologetically spoke against. Herodias disliked John intensely and set herself against him to harm him, but she could not convince Herod to touch him. Herod feared the anointing and the presence of the Lord in John's life. What a great example for us today.

We should be mindful not to speak or do any harm to those who are called by God for His purposes. John told Herod he broke the law by marrying Herodias, and as a result, he was put into prison. As he took this righteous stance, John was aware he would suffer the consequences but he took a stance anyway. He may not have understood what the cost would be, but He knew there would be a penalty for standing up for righteousness.

Consider for a moment the times you have spoken up because you saw unrighteousness or injustices. What was the cost? Did you lose some relationships? Were you black-listed and called names such as 'holier than thou'? A friend shared she is often referred to as 'holier than thou' because of her devotion and love for Jesus. I love this because she is such a reflection of Christ; her mere presence brings conviction and makes folks uncomfortable. People are uneasy not because she is preaching at them or to them, but by her mere presence, they become aware of their sinful lifestyles. She is a walking Bible these people can clearly read.

John was such an example. He reflected Jesus so completely Herodias was uncomfortable with him and wanted him destroyed. While he was imprisoned, John began to struggle with unbelief. In Matthew 11:2, he wondered if Jesus was the Messiah and sent his disciples to ask if He was the One or should they look for another. Jesus did not ignore John's question but told the disciples to tell John about His messages and miracles. Why was John in doubt after all his radical teachings and his declaration, "Behold the Lamb of God who takes away the sins of the world?" Sometimes, in our struggles, doubt about who God's ability, availability, and who He is, will creep into our hearts.

Remember, John's prophesies were mostly about the coming wrath. Jesus' ministry was not wrathful at all but filled with love, compassion, reconciliation, healing, and deliverance for the oppressed. John had probably believed, along with many Jews, that Jesus would set up an earthly kingdom. John's expectation of who Jesus was, and what He would do, did not match the reality of what Jesus did. Apparently, Jesus did not act like what John expected or hoped to see. This caused doubt to filter into his heart. What happens when your expectation of Jesus is not what He performs in your life? Do you become discouraged? Do you question the reality of who He is? Do you continue to trust Him, or do you become lukewarm in your devotion because you are disappointed?

Our expectations can cause us some setbacks. Generally, our expectations do not always match reality. When this happens, we need to make appropriate adjustments, but this can be difficult to do in moments of uncertainty. Jesus did not hold· this against John. He understood John's struggles. He understands your struggles in those moments when you have doubt and unbelief as it relates to trusting Him. He also understands you as you wonder if He will ever come to your rescue. As you grow in Him and come to know how truly faithful, He is, He reveals to you He is Lord even when you face tough times. He will do for you what He did for John. Jesus reminded John of what he already knew—He was the Messiah.

He pointed John back to the Word and reassured him He was the One who was to come. In doing this, Jesus comforted John, and John realized he had not prophesied in vain, nor did he misspeak about Jesus being Savior. John could anchor His hope in this truth. John understood the work he had begun preparing the way for the Savior of the world was complete. Jesus would take it from where he concluded and bring many more souls to the saving knowledge of God His Father.

The scripture tells us Herodias had waited with great anticipation for an opportunity to destroy John. Herod had a birthday party and Herodias' daughter danced for him. He was so enticed by her dancing he rashly offered her whatever she wanted, up to half of his kingdom. It is evident Herod struggled with fleshly desires. He was willing to give away half of his kingdom to a mere girl because she enticed him through a dance. This was a man who had problems with lust. When the girl inquired of her mother what she should ask for, Herodias did not care about owning half of Herod's kingdom. She did not even seem to notice her husband was entirely too enticed by her daughter. She overlooked everything because she was consumed with her revenge for John. Without hesitation, she told her to ask for the head of John the Baptist. Herod immediately felt remorseful, but since he had spoken so rashly, he honored his word and had John beheaded.

For thirty-plus years, John the Baptist was absolutely devoted to God. He knew nothing else but to follow totally after Him. He was focused on one thing and one thing only, and that was to assist in introducing Jesus to the world by being the mouthpiece that would usher Him in. I must speculate that John probably did not consider what the end result of his life would be. He probably never considered how his life would change upon Jesus' arrival. Yet, he made it clear when Jesus came, he would decrease so Jesus could increase. I wonder if he ever considered an early death as part of his future.

John knew he had fulfilled his assignment in the earth, and the purpose for which he was born was completed. He had not deviated from God's plans for his life. John entered eternity knowing his job was a job well done.

John's journey to his destiny was the wilderness and ultimately death. Jesus' journey to His destiny was the cross and ultimately death. These two men had much in common. They had totally surrendered their lives to God; they fulfilled their destinies. How grateful we are they did. When Jesus heard about John's death, He mourned him deeply. He profoundly felt this loss. Jesus understands our grief.

I close this chapter with some lessons from John's life.

- There are consequences for being radical and sold out to Jesus, but they are worth it.
- John fulfilled his assignment by not deviating from God's plan for his life.

- John prepared the hearts of the people by causing them to examine their own lives.
- He was blunt and confrontational in his teaching and made no apologies for it.
- John was the first earthly person to publicly acknowledge Jesus' ministry.
- He modeled the kind of devotion and commitment God is looking for from us.
- John was empowered by the Holy Spirit for his assignment.
- John boldly confronted sin. He did not care about peoples' status and position when he did but spoke the truth with power.
- John knew when and how to step aside when someone greater came along.
- He was filled with grace and humility.
- Though his ministry only lasted approximately two and half years, it was powerful and drew multitudes to Jesus.
- John said in John 3:30, He must increase, and I must decrease. He did not try to compete with Jesus but simply stepped aside when his season was over.

Jesus called John, "More than a prophet." He said among those born of women, there was not a greater prophet than John the Baptist. May Jesus one day also speak great things over us because we have completed our assignments on earth.

Remember, during your journey with Jesus, He will comfort you and walk with you through all the painful seasons of life. Do not let go of His hands, and never give up, because He is with you.

Like John the Baptist, you can TRUST Him.

ONLY TRUST HIM

Do you have a problem trusting people? How about God? There are some people like me who have experienced times when they doubted God's faithfulness. What I have discovered over the years is at times we have difficulty trusting God because the people in our lives have been untrustworthy. They did not honor their word or commitment to us. They were not there when we needed them the most. Some people lack trust because they were abandoned by their families or in their marriages.

Since people have abandoned us, we tend to believe God will also abandon us. It is especially easy for us to believe this because we cannot see God with the naked eye. We unconsciously reason if the ones we see daily can let us down and not keep their promises, how can we believe God will keep

His word? Unfortunately, some have developed a habit/mindset that they will be let down. Listen: God is not like man. Numbers 23:19 says, *"God is not a man that He should lie nor the son of man that He should repent, has He not said it and will He not do it?"* When God makes a promise, He is bound by it. He will never do anything contrary to His nature or His Word. His Word is binding and infallible. He cannot lie and He will not disown Himself. His nature is unchanging; therefore, when He speaks a word or gives you a promise it is as sure as dawn. Have you ever seen a time when night did not ultimately turn into a day or vice versa? Even after a major storm, the sun always shines again. This is our God—He is as sure as the changing seasons the earth experiences day by day.

Unlike man, God can be trusted. When we lack trust in Him it opens us up to attacks from the enemy. If we do not trust that God will provide for us, protect us, and help us, then we often experience fear as we face challenging situations. It is safe for me to conclude fear could probably be the deadliest weapon ever launched against us by the enemy. The feelings of dread, apprehension, anxiety, alarm, and fright we experience at times can be paralyzing. Fear causes us to lack confidence and to be timid in our dealings not only with people but at times even with God.

Hebrews says, "To come boldly before the throne of grace with confidence because He who has promised is faithful." When we lack trust, we feel anxious about situations and our life in general. Researchers say only eight percent of what we worry about will ever happen in our lifetime. This means ninety-two percent of what causes us fear will never happen to us.

The words 'fear not' appear approximately three hundred and sixty-five times in the Bible; one 'fear not' for each day of the year! It is evident God is trying to get something important across to us. We do not have to fear because we can trust Him. Think about times you experienced defeat because you feared; then as you looked back, you realized God would have given you the victory if only you had trusted Him.

There are also those who have been crippled by fear, and as a result, have not maximized their full potential because they did not trust or have confidence in God or themselves. We all have the tools to deal with fear—trusting God and His promises. Declare these words—I will not fear but only trust God. One of my favorite scriptures is Deuteronomy 31:6-8, *"Be strong and courageous, do not be afraid or terrified because of them, for the Lord your God goes with you; he will never leave you nor forsake you."* God gave me this scripture to declare over myself at a time when I felt fear over the magnitude of the assignments He was giving me.

When you are in a battle against fear, remember you already have the victory. Jesus has been victorious over the enemy on your behalf. Fear is from the devil. It is a spirit that is trying to intimidate you and keep you from trusting God. Fear may feel real but it is not real. Fear will take you to any destination you allow it to while trusting God will propel you to greater dimensions in your faith.

Soon after the September 11th attacks, I was scheduled to go to a meeting in Chicago a few days after these incidents. Paralyzing fear gripped me on the way to the airport. It was tormenting. I prayed and quoted scriptures but fear still hounded me. I could hear the voice of the Holy Spirit clearly saying to trust Him, but I struggled to grasp He was with me and would not allow disaster to come near me. We boarded the plane and the guy next to me went to the restroom several times before take-off, which was unusual, so it fed into my fear. All through this ordeal God continued to whisper to me to trust Him, but the voice of fear spoke more loudly than His voice.

I generally like takeoffs but not landings. As the plane taxied down the runway, my heart began to beat anxiously. I was terrified. Finally, in an urgent and loud voice, the Holy Spirit said, "Joan, get a hold of your fear before you give yourself a heart attack." Fear had me in such a vicious grip panic almost overcame me until God spoke firmly to me. This time, I heard Him over the fear and was able to get my emotions under control. It is obvious the plane did not crash since you are reading this book. In this crisis, all I needed to do was to listen to, and trust God.

Trusting God—why is this so hard even for someone like me who has served God since I was a child? Negative experiences in my life have eroded my trust in others, and I have projected these experiences onto the God who has never once shown me He could not be trusted. Because we cannot trust people this does not mean we cannot trust God. When God has a plan for your life and future, the enemy cannot take your life prematurely. So harness the fear! We must truly recognize God is trustworthy and His mercy for us is unfailing. Let's explore the life of Jacob and see how he went from living in fear to trusting God. He trusted God with his life as he faced his brother, Esau, who years earlier wanted to kill him.

Some of us have heard the story of these twin brothers. They struggled not only in the womb but also against each other in life.

When Isaac was old and his eyes were so weak that he could no longer see, he called for Esau his older son and said to him, "My son." "Here I am," he answered. Isaac said, "I am now an old man and don't know the day of my death. Now then, get your weapons—your quiver and bow—and go out to the open country to hunt some wild game for me. Prepare me the kind of tasty food I like and bring it to me to eat, so that I may give you my blessing before I die." Now Rebekah was listening as Isaac spoke to his son Esau. When Esau left for the open country to hunt game and bring it back, Rebekah said to her son Jacob, "Look, I overheard your father say to your brother, Esau, 'Bring me some game and prepare me some tasty food to eat, so that I may give you my blessing in the presence of the Lord before I die.' Now, my son, listen carefully and do what I tell you. Go out to the flock and bring me two choice young goats, so I can prepare some tasty food for your father, just the way he likes it. Then take it to your father to eat, so that he may give you his blessing before he dies."

Genesis 27:1-10 (NIV)

Prior to this event, Esau came from a hard day's work in the field and was hungry. Jacob had been cooking, and Esau asked him for some food. Jacob offered to give him the food in exchange for Esau's birthright. Esau was cavalier with his birthright and gave it to Jacob without a second thought about its significance for his future. Later, Jacob and his mother, Rebekah, plotted and stole the blessing, which during that century was reserved for the eldest son. The father would lay his hands on his firstborn son, and speak words of a successful and prosperous future for him, thus transferring the blessing and the responsibility of the family to him.

Although he had once been cavalier about his birthright, when Esau heard his blessing was stolen, it was a different story. Esau knew the power and value of the blessing and wanted to kill Jacob. As a result, with the help of his mother, Jacob ran away from home and ended up working for his uncle, Laban, for many years.

Rebekah knew God had already decided Jacob and not Esau, the eldest son, would be given the blessing and the mantle of leadership over the family. God told her in Genesis 25:23 that the older son would serve the younger one. God had chosen Jacob to carry on the lineage. There was no need to trick his brother since God already knew Esau's heart. When we do not know and understand the plans of God for our future, we often make our plans. These plans can lead us away from God's presence, cause us harm, or assist us in living mediocre lives. As we study Jacob's life, let's use his example as a roadmap for how not to make our own decisions, but to ask God for His input and plans for our destinies.

Jacob's name means supplanter or trickster. As we journey through his story, you will see he was in a battle against his own nature and struggled with trusting God, even though God showed him time and again He was with him. Rebekah had a favorite son, Jacob, while Isaac's favorite son was Esau. She expended all her efforts to help Jacob succeed, or so she thought. She wanted the best for Jacob and did what she felt was necessary to achieve her end results. It is evident she did not consider the harmful effect it was having on her other son, Esau, or the negative path she was setting Jacob on. She did not consider how her decisions would affect her husband who was simply following a long tradition of the blessing of God being transferred to the eldest son. Rebekah thought only of what she wanted and did not consider the division this would cause in her family. In all her scheming and plotting, she pitted one son against the other. She acted out of her emotions while not thinking about the consequences of her sin.

What Rebekah did not realize was that Jacob would not return home for approximately twenty-one years after running away. She never considered the personal cost to herself and her family. Both she and Isaac would miss seeing his wives and children. She probably assumed he was only leaving for a short time while Esau dealt with his anger against him. She missed being a constant part of his life for many years because she lacked trust in God's ability to take care of him. We see no mention in the Bible of Rebekah after this, and historians say by the time Jacob returned home she had already died.

There are some of you who, upon reading this will see a correlation within your own families. You have protected rather than challenged your children to become all God created them to be, defending them even when you knew they were wrong. You bailed them out time and again when they made wrong choices, never allowing them to face and deal with the consequences of their actions. As a result, you are dealing with heartaches because their lives are out of control. Some of them may have even lost their lives. Instead of helping them, you enabled behaviors that were not acceptable and have struggled with regret. Your greatest desire was to help them, yet they became worse and continued to make other harmful choices with their lives.

I can recount many stories of people in similar situations. Because of your love for your children, you find it hard to say and mean no. You have difficulty with seeing them struggle, so you step in to make the situations easier, not realizing the struggles were necessary to birth greatness in them. Jesus could not have redeemed us without dying on the cross. He had to struggle and suffer in order to gain victory and be glorified.

Think about the lifecycle of a butterfly. There are four stages in its life. Each stage has a different goal, therefore each stage although different, is equally necessary. In order to become an adult, the butterfly goes through a process called metamorphosis. This cycle can take from one month to a year depending on the type of butterfly. In the first stage, the lady butterfly lays an egg on a leaf, and about five days later it hatches and becomes a tiny worm-like creature. This is the second stage where it grows into a caterpillar (Larva) which looks like a worm.

The caterpillar is a very hungry creature and begins to eat

leaves and flowers. It first eats the leaves it was born on. Ponder that statement for a moment. The thing that supports the caterpillar's life becomes the thing it then feeds on. As our family members struggle with their issues, they will take, steal, and even lie to the very ones who are trying to help them get better. In this larva stage of the butterfly's development, it grows extremely fast because it eats a lot. It grows so fast it becomes too big for its skin which is shed about four times or more while it is growing. In this stage, all it does is eat, and then it enters stage three where it becomes a chrysalis (Pupa).

After it is done forming, the chrysalis takes on the color of the plants and trees around it, so it can blend in and not be seen by other animals. It is usually protected by a cocoon of silk. This is the protective stage where they are shielded from hurt. Just like the chrysalis is protected, so we often try to shield our family members from hurt by hiding what they are doing from others, or even pretending they are doing well while knowing they are in the grip of addictions. In this stage, the caterpillar is changing and will rest for a season.

It is during the fourth stage the caterpillar becomes the butterfly. Scientists explain the butterfly is supposed to struggle to emerge from its cocoon. The struggle to push its way through the tiny opening, to free itself from its chrysalis, is an essential step in strengthening its wings. As it struggles, it begins to pump blood into its wings in order to get them working and flapping so it can fly. The fluids in the butterfly's body are transferred to its wings, and only in that way can it be ready to fly. If the butterfly is helped at any point, the blood does not fill the wings and the butterfly will die because it cannot fly to feed itself. Within three to four hours the butterfly masters flying and begins searching for a mate in order to reproduce.

My point in sharing this example is this—in the struggles of life we become stronger. Struggles are necessary to make us into the person we are to become. Without struggles we will never attain our fullest potential; we will never learn to fly. When we attempt to keep our loved ones from going through the struggles of life, whether they are a result of their own choices or because God is allowing a season of difficulty in their lives, we do them a disservice.

Character is built and refined during the difficult seasons of life. If we don't learn how to persevere through these difficulties, we will miss opportunities to know God and experience the richness of His presence in our lives. Just like the butterfly, struggles allow you to attain the highest heights in life. Let's return to the story of Jacob who was being developed like this butterfly.

The Journey Home

After being gone for many years, Jacob decided it was time to return home and face his past, and his brother Esau. On his previous journey away from home, he met an angel and God gave him some significant promises for his life. In Genesis 28:13-15, God said, *"I am the Lord, the God of Abraham your father and the God of Isaac. The land on which you lie I will give to you and your offspring. Your offspring will be like the dust of the earth, and you shall spread abroad to the west and to the east, to the north and to the south, and in you and your offspring shall all the families of earth be blessed. Behold I am with you and will keep you wherever you go, and will bring you back to this land. For I will not leave you until I have done what I have promised you."* Even with all these promises Jacob was still fearful. He feared facing Esau and began plotting how to overcome him instead of asking God for help.

It is ironic he had previously plotted with his mother to steal the blessing, and now he is plotting to get Esau to receive him in peace. This sounds a bit like some of us who are trying to work out our plans in an attempt to combat our fears. The only way to combat fear is to face it head-on and do battle against it.

When we are overcome with fear it is hard to think clearly and harder still to hear God. Yet, in spite of his fear, it was still Jacob who took the initiative to go and face Esau and deal with the issues between them. As he prepared to meet Esau he did the most important thing—he prayed and reminded God of His promises to him. Jacob acknowledged his unworthiness and acknowledged God's kindness and faithfulness to him. He reminded God of His Word—He would prosper him, and he asked God to save him. After this intense prayer, Jacob began to hatch a plan to pacify Esau. He had prayed but still doubted. Sound familiar? He sought God, yet it appeared he did not accept the reassurance God had this, and his life, under His control so he came up with his own plan of action.

His plan was to give Esau a gift of approximately five

hundred and eighty animals. Jacob sent his servants to Esau with these gifts and instructions on what to say. Jacob continued with his plotting and planning as before. Next, he sent his wives and children ahead of him and was entirely alone. Having done everything in his own strength, he spent the night at the camp. It is evident Jacob felt he had done all that was necessary to get the best of Esau. He does not seem to be aware God was after his heart, God wanted to make a change in his life. It is worth noting the moment he was alone was when God showed up to do a deep cleansing work in his heart.

God will usually deal with the issues in our hearts when we are alone with Him. Why? Because it is personal! God does not want to expose our hidden struggles, fear, or shame. He wants to teach us how to be victorious over every hidden struggle. Jacob's day of reckoning and deliverance had come. Jacob could not ultimately become the person he was created to be without God humbling him, and remaking him into something better. Likewise, God is pursuing us so He can remake us into the image of His Son.

Face-to-Face with God

When Jacob was alone was the time for God to choose to deal with his nature, character, and the issues of his heart.

So Jacob was left alone, and a man wrestled with him till daybreak. When the man saw that he could not overpower him, he touched the socket of Jacob's hip so that his hip was wrenched as he wrestled with the man. Then the man said, "Let me go, for it is daybreak." But Jacob replied, "I will not let you go unless you bless me." Genesis 32:24-26 (NIV)

The scripture says a man wrestled with Jacob. Let's examine this. Why did the man wrestle with Jacob instead of speaking to him? God recognized Jacob could not or would not hear Him, since he was in the grip of fear and his own plans.

The word wrestle means he struggled, grappled, and strived against the man who could not overpower him. That is an amazing statement because we know angels are strong beings. This man was an angel who touched Jacob's hip and his hip was wrenched. He told Jacob to let him go since it was daybreak. How could this angel not get free from Jacob's grip when Jacob, as a mere human, did not have his level of power and strength? God gave Jacob the strength to hang on to the angel because He was at work in Jacob's life.

We have heard stories of people with supernatural strength when loved ones are in crisis. Jacob was in a crisis place in his life, so his hold was unbelievable. He recognized the change he needed was in his grasp and he would not let go of Him. He wrestled all night without realizing until daybreak just who he was fighting against. He was wrestling not against an angel but the pre-incarnate Messiah, Jesus!

As soon as Jacob realized he was fighting against God, he stopped wrestling and surrendered to Him. He yielded his heart and life. Jacob recognized he could not achieve anything worthwhile by wrestling against the One who had his blessings. We cannot get anything from God by struggling and resisting Him but only by surrendering. Jacob said to the angel, "I will not let you go until you bless me." Jacob realized the One he had been fighting against had the blessings he needed for his life to change.

I do not believe Jacob was asking for material blessings. He already had those in abundance. God had already given him a large family and great wealth. What then was he asking for? Remember, he was dealing with great fear as he prepared to meet Esau. It's possible he was asking for help to conquer his fear as he faced Esau. He could have been asking for God to spare his life. He had been a man without peace in his heart for a long time due to the situation with Esau, followed by his dealings with his uncle Laban.

Jacob needed something that had greater eternal value. He needed God to take over and rule his life. In response, the angel asked him this question. What is your name? Your name in that century meant something. It still means something today, which is why parents should be careful what they name their children. Your name spoke of your nature and character.

His name Jacob, as was previously mentioned, meant trickster and supplanter but that was not who he was created to be. He had allowed himself to become less than God intended by making choices that were not in alignment with God's will for his life. To become who he was created to be means he needed a name change, a new identity. The angel renamed him Israel meaning—God rules, God fights, or God contends. This new name says God, not Jacob was in control.

In the process of changing his name, God allowed him to strive to overcome his old nature. His old name was supplanted in that intense fight and replaced with a new identity in Christ. He moved into a new season of blessings, after being humbled by his experience. God marked him—he stamped him with a limp that would be a reminder throughout his life of his God encounter. I believe this would keep him from returning to his old self and serve as a reminder God was in absolute control of his future.

In Peniel, Jacob met God and was forever changed. Peniel means the face of God. Jacob met God face-to-face and lived.

The Meeting

After all the anxiety, fear, plotting, and planning, Jacob meets Esau. He had expected negative consequences from Esau, but Esau ran to him, embraced him, threw his arms around his neck, and kissed him. You have to wonder how many years had passed since Esau had forgiven Jacob. Jacob had stayed away from his family for years and was filled with fear, worries, and concerns when he finally headed home, not knowing he was already forgiven. Esau had changed over the years and was gracious, loving, and thoughtful. He had made plans to care for Jacob and his family as they traveled.

Esau did not want or need any of Jacob's animals. God had

also blessed him abundantly because he was Isaac's seed, even though he was not chosen to lead the family into the future. It is possible, based on Esau's welcome Jacob could have gone home years earlier. It is also possible he could have had time with his mother before she died. Yet he did not, because he was unsure of the reception he would receive upon his arrival. God had already taken care of his future and all he needed to do was to trust Him. We must also trust Him.

Think about times in your life when you have worried needlessly. The sleepless nights you have spent worrying about a situation in the family, on the job, in the marriage, or about your health. Yet when the report came it was not as devastating as expected. Some of us have been down this path. There have been times when I have waited on a doctor's report and just could not find my place of peace. There have also been seasons when I have labored in prayer over the health of loved ones and friends and dreaded hearing bad news.

I had a friend who faced a shocking diagnosis, and we labored in prayer for this dear woman. There were times when I prayed in great desperation that God would spare her life. She had been a great friend and intercessor for me and the ministries, and I did not want to lose this valuable gift. I prayed in faith often, but there were also times I prayed while fear was hounding me because it looked as if she would not survive. The stress was tangible at times.

We must, however, find our peace in God during difficult struggles. How? By remembering He is faithful to His promises, and He can be trusted; by spending time in His presence seeking His peace; by gathering people around you who will stand in the gap for you and pray with you; and by speaking related scriptures over yourself during times of unrest. Jacob encountered God and had many promises spoken over his life yet struggled with believing all would be well when he met with Esau face to face. God went ahead of him, smoothed out the crooked places, and made his pathway easy.

At the conclusion of the embrace and kiss, Esau offered to travel with Jacob until he reached home but Jacob refused his help. Esau then offered for his men to help Jacob with his children and all his cattle, but again Jacob refused. What I see taking place is Esau had experienced a genuine heart transformation. He no longer had hard feelings or murderous intentions toward his brother. He had released the past, forgiven the offenses, and moved on with his life, but Jacob still doubted him. Remember on the journey away from home Jacob encountered God and received many promises. Right before meeting Esau he once again encountered God and was reassured about the great plans for his future, but it still had not sunken in that God would take care of him.

Seeing Esau's reaction should have been a clear indication God had moved in his situation, but he still hesitated. Jacob told Esau he and all his children would travel slowly and see him on Mount Seir; however, he had no intention of reconnecting with Esau, despite giving the promise. The moment Esau left, Jacob with a flash of his old nature, went to live in Succoth and not Mount Seir as he had indicated to Esau. It is evident God still needed to do more work in Jacob's heart. There was still a level of fear and lack of faith in God's promises. Maybe his doubt had some justification since he had been away from Esau for many years. God, however, had faithfully watched over him throughout his life and would not fail him now. He needed to trust God more.

Upon realizing Esau did not mean him any harm or want his gifts, Jacob said something profound, "To see your face is like seeing the face of God." This was Jacob's experience with Peniel. Jacob saw God face-to-face and lived. When he saw Esau face-to-face and survived the encounter it was a reminder God could be trusted with his life. He lived!

How do you deal with fear? Has it paralyzed you? Does it keep you from believing God has a future filled with hope and blessings for you? Does fear keep you from believing and trusting God? Has the fear of being hurt or rejected kept you from developing some important, lifelong relationships? Or is afraid of the unknown keeping you from being bold in your faith and moving toward the destiny God birthed in you? I can say conclusively people can cause you to experience more fear than you would normally feel.

As the team and I have prepared to undertake ministry and mission trips to various parts of the world, people will attempt to plant doubt in our minds about the possible dangers and potential outcomes in our lives. If we are not careful, we can absorb their fears and not move into what God has for us. I remind them the same faithful God who keeps us safe in the USA, where many deaths occur regularly, is the same God who will keep us safe as we trust Him in other parts of the world. Have you discovered yet you are safest in the center of God's will for your life? Once you put your hands to the plow in hopes of making a difference for God, do not look back (Luke 9:62). He will keep you safe because the enemy will not be allowed to take your life prematurely.

Do not take on other's fears for you have enough of your own to master. And don't allow all the false evidence around you to cause you to believe the wrong things/reports. In the presence of fear, allow faith to rise because, in the presence of God, fear will always vanish. Faith and trust are more powerful than fear. Remember, fear originates from the devil while faith comes from a loving God who wants His children to be at peace. Every day, you and I get to choose where we will live, either in faith or in fear. Remember, there are three hundred and sixty-five 'fear not' in the Bible. Declare over yourself God has not given you a spirit of fear, but of power, love, and a sound mind (2 Timothy 1:7). Keep declaring these words until they become as real to you as the breath you breathe. I challenge you as I challenge myself regularly, choose faith over fear and you will always be victorious.

As I conclude this book, my goal is to remind you that you have support on every side. Your Savior, Jesus, has been and will always be with you throughout your journey. Not once was He ever unaware of where you are nor has He ever taken His eyes from you. Not once has He heard your cries for help and ignored them. When others do not see or hear you, God does. When people overlook you because they assume you have no value, know you are highly valued in God's eyes. I make this statement often, "If you were the only person on the planet, God would still have sent His precious Son, Jesus, to die for you because you are valuable and special to Him."

Jesus redeemed you by shedding His blood on Calvary, and

daily He redeems your life from destruction. I believe we will be amazed when we meet Jesus face-to-face and discover how many times He has stepped into our lives and rescued us from disasters. When no one is available to pick up your broken pieces, Jesus is there. In the midnight hours, when you are fearful, in pain, or brokenhearted, the Lover of your soul, Jesus, is only a call away. He redeemed you from eternal damnation and gave you a place in eternity. He continually redeems your life from destruction, so you can fulfill all He wants you to accomplish in the earth. You can trust Him.

Remember, He will protect and keep you safe time and again as you continue to anchor your hope and TRUST in Him.

Do not let go of Him when times are painful and dark; He is a very present help in times of trouble. Like Jacob, you can TRUST Him.

A PRAYER—TRUSTING GOD

~

Lord, there are seasons when I wonder where You are. Are You with me? Do You hear me? Do You see my distress? Yet, in other seasons, I am reminded You have been with me all along and I can trust You. I remember You have seen me through one difficulty after another. I remember when I thought I would not make it, You showed me I could and would.

When I look back over my life, I am amazed at the many things I have overcome. In my brokenness when I reached for You, You were always there to comfort me. Why then do I struggle with believing You? Why do I lack faith in Your promises? Why do I allow myself to become burdened with fear? Why do I so quickly forget You are with me? Is it because I fail to trust You in all things? Remind me You have been my anchor in every stormy event in my life. You have been my rock and my safe place—my place of refuge from the storms. Help me to trust wholly in You at all times.

Hear my voice when I call, Lord; be merciful to me and answer me. My heart says of you, "Seek his face!" Your face, Lord, I will seek. Do not hide your face from me, do not turn your servant away in anger; you have been my helper. Do not reject me or forsake me, God my Savior. Though my father and mother forsake me, the Lord will receive me. Teach me your way, Lord; lead me in a straight path. I remain confident of this; I will see the goodness of the Lord in the land of the living. Wait for the Lord; be strong and take heart and wait for the Lord.

Psalm 27:7-14 (NIV)

Father, I am confident as I trust You more and more, I will discover Your goodness is always with me and I will experience this goodness for the rest of my life. Father, as I wait on You, teach me how to take heart in every trying situation because You are with me and You are trustworthy.

Lord, thank You that You do REMEMBER ME. Thank You for redeeming me from every pit I have been in, even those of my own making. You have been faithful, steadfast, and sure. I will remember Your goodness all the days of my life. Thank You for redeeming me from every trouble, unharmed. I CAN TRUST YOU.

Amen – So Be It!

A PRAYER FOR SALVATION

Father, I acknowledge You sent Jesus into the world to die for my sins. I believe He is Your Son; that He was born of a virgin, and He died and rose from the dead for my sins. I acknowledge I have sinned and fallen short of Your standards, and I ask You to forgive me. I invite Jesus to come into my heart because the Bible says He is the way, truth, and life, and no man comes to the Father but by Him. Father, I am coming to You in the precious name of Your Son, Jesus. I thank You for saving me and setting me free, in Jesus' name.

Amen - So Be It!

I MUST PRAY!

A GUIDE TO A POWERFUL PRAYER LIFE

"Consider this, since you schedule many things, why not schedule the most important thing—time with God."

There are people who struggle with knowing how to pray, and what to pray for when they desire to commune with God. As a result of these uncertainties, some do not devote a great deal of time or concerted effort to prayer. There are also those who will reason, why pray at all because they have not received immediate responses to their prayers. Others may feel inadequate when praying so they do not seek after God consistently. People are at times intimidated when hearing others pray, and as a result, will not venture to pray in group settings. These trying situations and others have caused many people not to pursue God. At times it is hard to stay focused when praying because we may be conscious about some of these things. Also, because of a lack of consistency in prayer some have not yet discovered the joy, peace, hope, and contentment, they can experience each time they pray. Whatever has hindered your prayer walk, I encourage you to set it aside so you can come to know God in a more powerful and intimate way. This depth of intimacy can only be achieved through prayer.

I MUST pray, is a challenge to all of us. It reminds us prayer is not optional but must become central in our lives. As you read in the previous chapter, prayer was a MUST in the life of Jesus as He walked the earth. It was not optional to Him but was the main thing that kept Him on course while pursuing His destiny. Prayer kept Him steady and focused all the way to the cross.

After observing the consistent prayer life of Jesus and all He accomplished, the disciples realized that this was the key to success in their earthly assignments. They recognized that since prayer was essential to Jesus, it was also essential to them, so they asked Him to teach them to pray. There is no shame in admitting you need help in connecting to God in a more real, personal, and powerful way. You also have the same access to Jesus to ask Him to teach you how to pray. He will teach you so you can connect with the Godhead at any time and in all situations.

I want to devote this chapter to assisting you in developing a rich, full, and sustainable prayer life.

A close friend shared with me that over the years she had observed that many believers do not know how to pray effectively. As they pray, some do not feel they are praying correctly. When asked to pray, others will either pray the same rehearsed prayers or will pray something entirely different from what they were asked. I believe it is extremely important we pray as the Holy Spirit leads, and when we are asked to lead a specific prayer topic, it is important we pray what we are asked. If someone asks you to pray for sickness in their body, be sure to pray for God to heal them and not for the problems going on in the world.

Have you discovered that there are scriptures to cover every challenging situation you and others might be facing? When you know the Word, you can pray the Word. Praying the Word ensures you always know what to say to receive the right results. Praying the Word will also have an eternal and everlasting impact in the lives of people. Remember this—God did not leave us without the answers and the necessary tools to be successful in life. He has filled us with the Holy Spirit, who is our Teacher, for a reason. With the help of the Holy Spirit, we can attain what seems unattainable and have victory over everyday challenges. The challenge is we must get to know God's Word and spend time learning the ways and acts of the Holy Spirit. This equipping will ensure you are never uncomfortable when asked to pray, or when you see a need that requires God's intervention.

In the model prayer, Jesus taught the disciples some key elements that ensured effectiveness in their prayer life. As I highlight various prayer points, I pray you also find the answers you need to have both an effective and satisfying prayer life. Let's look at this prayer to glean what is needed to enrich our encounters with the Father.

H e said to them, "This, then, is how you should pray: "'Our Father in heaven, hallowed be your name, your kingdom come, your will be done, on earth as it is in heaven. Give us today our daily bread. And forgive us our debts, as we also have forgiven our debtors. And lead us not into temptation, but deliver us from the evil one. Matthew 6:9-13 (NIV)

T he first thing I want to point out is that the closing statement, "for thine is the kingdom and the power, and the glory, forever," is not a part of the original prayer. This closing is called a doxology and was added by Christians of the early Church who lived in the eastern half of the Roman Empire. In the Bible, we find this practice of concluding prayers with a short, hymn-like verse that exalts the glory of God. This was known as a climactic doxology with a passionate declaration of God's sovereignty.

In this model prayer are some key prayer points that will help us to obtain the things for which we are praying. We must have the right attitude when approaching God. Our hearts must be filled with thankfulness. We must worship Him telling of the amazing things He has done and all His wonderful attributes. Asking for forgiveness for ourselves and others must become an essential part of our prayer time. Remember to ask God to release you from temptations and to keep evil influences away from you.

In this model prayer, you will also find other key elements designed to strengthen your prayer life. Let's explore these eight things that will lead us to victory:

- Knowing your position in God
- A private place to meet with God
- An attitude of praise/worship
- God's presence and will revealed
- God will provide for every need
- God will pardon and forgive you
- God will protect you
- God is glorious and powerful

Purchase your copy now by clicking the link or visiting our website.

JOAN E. MURRAY

I MUST PRAY!

www.jemmuniquegifts.com

NOTES:

Chapters 1-11
    Zondervan Bible Commentary
    FF Bruce, General Edition
    (Grand Rapids, MI)

Chapters 1-11
    Vine's Expository Dictionary
    Edited by Stephen D. Renn
    Hendrickson Publishers Marketing LLC

Chapters 1-11
    All the Books and Chapters of the Bible
    1972, Zondervan Publishing House
    Grand Rapids, MI

NOTES:

Chapters 1-11

The Illustrated Dictionary & Concordance of the Bible
General Editor, Geoffrey Wigoder, PH.D.
Sterling Publishing Co. Inc., New York

Chapters 2, 6, 7, 11

Every Man in the Bible
Larry Richards
Illustrated by Paul Gross
Thomas Nelson Publishers
Nashville, TN
When God Winks at You by Squire Rushnell
Thomas Nelson Publishers, ©2006

Chapters 1-11

Dictionary-Merriam-Webster.com Thesaurus, Merriam-Webster,
https://www.merriam-webster.com/thesaurus/dictionary
Lifecycle of a Butterfly
The Academy of Natural Sciences
Of Drexel University
Philadelphia, Pennsylvania

ABOUT THE AUTHOR

Joan Murray is committed to helping people discover their destinies. She is the founder and CEO of Joan Murray Ministries and Seeds of Hope Worldwide Missions. Joan is dedicated to teaching, training, equipping, and helping people with various life struggles.

Joan is a minister, Bible teacher, author, and missionary. She has traveled extensively throughout the United States and internationally sharing the gospel message and serving the needs of the oppressed. Joan currently resides in Houston, Texas.

If you would like to know more about Joan Murray Ministries or Seeds of Hope Worldwide Missions, please get in touch with us at:

Joan Murray Ministries & Seeds Of Hope Worldwide Missions
26340 FM 1736
Waller, TX 77848
281-398-2501
email: jmmcontactus@gmail.com
website: www.jemmuniquegift.com
website: www.joanmurrayministries.org

Changing Lives Through the Power and Truth of God's Word.

www.ingramcontent.com/pod-product-compliance
Lightning Source LLC
Chambersburg PA
CBHW061145120626
46546CB00005B/1943